SILENT
SCREAM

SILENT SCREAM

Josh Cannon

JOHN MURRAY

First published in Great Britain in 2008 by John Murray (Publishers)
An Hachette Livre UK company

1

© Josh Cannon 2008

A CIP catalogue record for this title is available from the British Library

Hardback ISBN 978-0-7195-2078-5
Trade paperback ISBN 978-0-7195-2088-4

Typeset in 12/15 pt Sabon by Servis Filmsetting Ltd, Manchester
Printed and bound by Clays Ltd, St Ives plc

John Murray policy is to use papers that are natural, renewable and recyclable products and made from wood grown in sustainable forests. The logging and manufacturing processes are expected to conform to the environmental regulations of the country of origin.

John Murray (Publishers)
338 Euston Road
London NW1 3BH

www.johnmurray.co.uk

To my beautiful son and to M for bringing me back from the dead

Author's Note

I have from the outset been determined not to soften or minimise the events depicted in this book in any way. Sexual abuse (and the ensuing addictions, eating disorders and self-mutilation) is a messy, violent and horrific subject. Rather than sugar-coat it in order to produce 'acceptable' reading material, I have endeavoured to depict the incidents of abuse and violence as vividly as they existed for me. While I'm deeply grateful to my publishers for supporting me in this, it would be irresponsible of me not to warn readers that certain passages may be very triggering to those who have undergone similar traumas. Please do not read this book if you feel unequipped to do so safely.

JC

joshcannon@mac.com

This is a true story, although some
identities have been disguised.

God won't be in life like a bright morning.
We have to go down into the shaft
And through the hard work of mining
Bring up the earth's abundance.
We have to stand hunched over
And in tunnels dig him out.

– Rainer Maria Rilke

It strikes me as I walk through my front door that, much to my dismay, there are an awful lot of ways to end my life. Like a fat kid in Baskin-Robbins, there are a plethora of tempting solutions to the pain I'm in. I've spent the past six months locked in secure mental institutions and discussed suicide with shrinks, schizophrenics, manic depressives, anorexics and plain old-fashioned lunatics, but I still never imagined there would be quite so many choices available.

In fact I'm now even more depressed at the amount of effort required to narrow down the options to a single, tidy way out. I've tried hanging a couple of times but was either found and cut down, or just bottled out at the thought of pissing myself, possibly decapitating myself or being found with eyes bulging out like a rapist. I'm kind of vain like that.

Truth is, although I'm barely in a position to know what that word means any more, I simply want an easy, quick and sure way to die. Hand on heart, I can say that I've had enough of everything. I feel like a surly teenager who's crossed that subtle line from teen angst to the 'holy shit, life really *is* that bad' mentality. I'll be leaving behind a beautiful three year-old son, a wife of four years who's sexy, compassionate and supportive, and a myriad of friends who profess to love me. I have money in the bank, a career I'm passionate about and I'm good-looking. I'm not bad in bed, in decent physical shape, debt-free, live in a nice part of town, went to the right schools, got a first-rate degree in psychology (seriously), give to charity, bathe every day, can sit through a Shakespeare play and understand most of what the fuck's going on, and I don't have ginger hair. And I'm finally in that place where I'm willing to turn away from all that and eagerly stumble down into the underworld in a fit of hideous self-pity and wanton self-hatred.

I just wish it were a bit easier to make the final jump (no pun intended). Even if I can narrow down the choice a bit, there is a lot of homework necessary if I'm to do it correctly (see the table below of weight to drop ratio under hanging, for example). Here are a few suggestions (but certainly not the complete list) I came up with and am happy to share with you:

- 1. Poison: cyanide, aspirin, paracetamol, sleeping tablets, alcohol, water, bleach, insulin (injected), petrol (in lungs/injected), insecticide, phosphine gas, potassium chloride, nitrogen gas (or other inert gas), nitrous oxide, carbon monoxide, chlorine gas, hydrazine, chloroform, digitalis, yew, mexerein, atropine, oleander, death cap, ricin, colchicine, aconitine, cicutoxin, coniine, oenanthetoxin, nicotine, iron, cocaine, LSD, heroin, rotenone, mercury, amobarbital, butabarbital, codeine (combined with aspirin), diazepam, flurazepam, gluthethimide, chloral hydrate, hydromorphone, meprobamate, methyprylon, meperidine, methadone, morphine, phenobarbital, secobarbital, propoxyphene, pentobarbital

- 2. Asphyxiation

- 3. Hanging; please see the handy table below on how to do it quickly and without decapitation (can be most upsetting for the funeral parlour not to mention the discoverer)

Culprit's Weight	Drop
14 stone (196 lb)	8ft 0in
13½ stone (189 lb)	8ft 2in
13 stone (182 lb)	8ft 4in
12½ stone (175 lb)	8ft 6in
12 stone (168 lb)	8ft 8in
11½ stone (161 lb)	8ft 10in
11 stone (154 lb)	9ft 0in
10½ stone (147 lb)	9ft 2in
10 stone (140 lb)	9ft 4in
9½ stone (133 lb)	9ft 6in
9 stone (126 lb)	9ft 8in
8½ stone (119 lb)	9ft 10in
8 stone (112 lb)	10ft 0in

- 4. Jumping off buildings
- 5. Slitting wrists (make sure you leave your arms in a bowl of ice for at least an hour and then cut vertically from the inside of the elbow down to the palm and remember you're aiming for at least 1cm depth)
- 6. Bullet
- 7. Air in veins (actually this one is a myth)
- 8. Decapitation (head out of a fast-moving train window is best since guillotines are hard to find)
- 9. Disembowelment
- 10. Drowning
- 11. Electrocution
- 12. Explosives
- 13. Freezing to death (hypothermia)
- 14. Jumping in front of trains
- 15. Self-immolation (setting fire to yourself)
- 16. Starving to death
- 17. Driving into bridge support at 100mph (but I want to leave my big-ass BMW to my buddy Greg so I can discount this one)
- 18. Shotgun
- 19. Enlist (a bit silly, and the climate in Iraq isn't really my scene)

- 20. Pencils up your nose, bang down on table (an urban legend alas – your frontal lobes are purely optional and the pain would be excruciating with no return to sender at the end of it)

- 21. Getting someone to murder you

- 22. Scuba diving (lungs bursting by rising 30 metres without exhaling, the bends)

- 23. Dehydration

- 24. Crushing

- 25. Heatstroke

- 26. Acid bath

- 27. Being eaten alive

- 28. AIDS

- 29. Auto-decapitation by car (kneel by the road as if tying your shoelaces then calmly fall forward head first into the oncoming car/truck)

After sitting with all the options swirling around in my head and smoking a number of cigarettes which are vital to good decision-making, I've decided to use the humble razor blade. It feels such a release to make the decision. I know it can take up to eight hours to bleed out but I've sent my wife and son to stay with my in-laws in France and have two weeks at home on my own.

Everyone who is close to me thinks I am still in a psychiatric hospital in Oxfordshire. They've released me after a couple of weeks of consistently good behaviour. My skills at manipulation have been honed to a fine art over the years, and the medical staff there genuinely think I'm on the road to recovery, the stupid bastards. I'm sure the fact that my insurance company has stopped paying the bills also helped them in their decision-making process. I carefully avoided signing any data release forms so the only person who knows I'm out will be my GP and even he won't find out until they send him a letter in a few days, by which time I'll no doubt be turning green and beginning to smell quite badly.

I'm sorted.

I take a deep breath and exhale slowly. I've chosen my way out and covered all my bases. Now I need to move on to stage 3.

First thing I have to do is write my notes. I'm not going to put them in here because they're personal and, to be honest, a little cheesy. I make sure my best friend Ed gets an e-mail detailing my computer password, bank account details and other boring domestic stuff. I also give him details about who and who not to invite to the funeral and some kind words about not blaming himself and how much I love him. The usual crap. I know he's in the Caribbean on business where it's the middle of the night and he won't be checking e-mails until the morning, if at all.

Then I write to my wife Jessica. This one takes an age to write even though it is barely a page long. I know she'll never forgive me, but frankly I'm past caring.

Daniel, my little three-year-old boy, I leave until last. I figure Jess can give it to him in a few years. It is two words in the middle of a page of Smythson's finest. 'Forgive me.' Jesus Christ, I'm in a Merchant Ivory production.

I walk down to Threshers and buy a big bag of ice and some more cigarettes. Then I go next door to the chemist and buy my blades.

I'm at home and have tipped the ice into the bathroom sink. I am running a bath, all hot water, and I've downed half a dozen clonazepam, surely one of the pharmaceutical industry's finest creations. Now I'm going to put my arms into the ice and sit in a nice hot bath for at least an hour which will no doubt make it difficult to type but I'll do my best.

Seventy minutes later and it is definitely harder to think straight now. Each word seems to take at least a minute to type. The ice has really done its job though. I have foot-long cuts down both arms. Way more blood than I'd thought possible, but Sony makes great computers and my little Vaio seems to be able to deal with the mess. Should have looked for a sponsorship deal. Shake 'n' Vac should take care of the carpet when they return.

I'm very drowsy. And cold. Fuck. Mozart's Jupiter symphony is on the stereo . . . It's nice . . . So happy to go.

Goodbye, Danny.

It is more than a little irritating to own up to the fact that the only reason I'm still here to write this is because some cunt decided he couldn't live without 24/7 access to his e-mail and invented those fucking BlackBerries.

Ed forgot to switch his mobile off after getting into bed at some fancy hotel in Jamaica. At 3 a.m. it belched out the ping for an incoming e-mail and for better or worse he got his lazy ass out of bed and grabbed it. I guess he was going to turn it off and try to get a decent night's sleep until he saw the subject line and who it was from.

When you get a middle-of-the-night e-mail from a friend you haven't heard from in a while and the subject is: 'I'm sorry to do this to you', the chances are, unless you're a heartless bastard, you'll open it. Even at three in the morning.

Ed is many things, but what he is not is a heartless bastard.

He is a billionaire with a heart of gold – a kind of Mother Teresa with a cock, jacked up with a shit load of steroids. He is twice my age, bald, grew up in a trailer park somewhere in upstate New York, and I absolutely love him. He is the father I had always dreamed of having. And earning over £10 million a month gives him the ability to make miracles happen for those less fortunate. He read my e-mail, called the emergency services in London and booked himself on to the next flight out of Jamaica.

My friend Ed saved my life and then he gave me a shot at a new one. He came to my house, packed a bag, pulled enough strings to have me discharged from hospital and into his care and twelve hours later he personally put me on to a plane to Phoenix where, according to him, I would find 'the safest place in the world'. A place I'd long given up any hope of ever finding.

As I boarded the plane the stewardess directed me upstairs into the business-class section. That's Ed for you.

I endured the twelve-hour flight to Phoenix International Airport by lying down in my fully flat bed, curling up into a ball and avoiding all possible communication with the stewardess. When I got to the airport I had been told by Ed to look for a driver called Ray who would be wearing a badge with a large 'R' on it. This badge was the only clue to those out of the loop as to where I was going: the Refuge, a secure mental facility in the middle of the Arizona desert that Ed told me he had been to twelve years previously.

I saw Ray immediately after clearing customs. He was tall, old and had leathery, wrinkled dark skin that could only come from too many years living in a desert climate. I was guessing he didn't moisturise. The 'R' was purple and

displayed discreetly on the lapel of his khaki jacket. I
nodded once to him, gave him my solitary bag and
followed him to his SUV in the car park. As we walked I
ripped off the nicotine patch that British Airways'
ridiculous anti-smoking policy had forced me to wear and
sucked greedily on a Marlboro. Ray loaded my bag into
the boot and held the passenger door open for me. He
adjusted his Stetson and started to chat about the weather
while I finished my smoke – smoking in the car was
apparently not an option.

I had lost the will to live a long time ago. I was in a foreign
country thousands of miles from what was familiar to me,
depressed beyond belief and angrier than I'd ever thought
possible. Small talk was just not on my agenda. I told him
to shut the fuck up and drive, jumped in the back and
pretended to fall asleep.

The Refuge is located in a total shithole town called
Friedburg about twenty minutes from Phoenix. Friedburg
is a small, dusty town in the middle of the desert where
it reaches 120°F (49°C) for several months of the year. It
has the three 'C's of any halfway authentic bumfuck
settlement near the desert: Cactuses, Coyotes and
Christianity.

Everyone smiles, prays and says hello as they pass you.
They all drive vast pick-up trucks, and they still believe
cowboys are something to aspire to (I guess that's a fourth
C). Most of the cowboys I've seen here are over 250

pounds and spend their days drinking beer and trying to rope steers at the rodeo every weekend. It's the horses I feel sorry for.

On the flight over, it became very clear that this place was without question the last house on the block for me. Or to continue in the cowboy vein, my last chance saloon.

I found myself at thirty, a husband and father. The world was at my feet as I was constantly being told, and yet I was in so much pain that within the last eight months I had tried three times to kill myself, been sectioned and incarcerated by the health authorities in Oxfordshire, and had been completely broken apart and decimated by my demons.

If it had not been for Ed and his goddamn BlackBerry those demons would have won the battle hands down. God knows they still might. The truth is, I was terrified of going to this place. I had no idea what to expect, and was here only because I trusted Ed more than anyone else I knew. I believed he and I were friends and hoped desperately that he wouldn't let me down. I was counting on him.

———

Ed used to drink a lot. He also liked to snort vast quantities of coke. After a drinking career spanning nearly thirty years he himself surrendered to the Refuge in 1994. He has not taken a drink or a drug since. The week before enrolling in rehab he was in Spain at one of his many houses. He'd been out partying with clients and had left the bar in his brand-new Porsche GT. As he approached one of the busiest social scenes in Barcelona he lost control of the car and flipped it, skidding over 100 yards along what should have been a crowded pavement at that time of night. For some reason he still can't figure out, the area was almost deserted. The bars and restaurants that on a normal summer's night have hundreds of people outside drinking, smoking and flirting were standing empty. He hit no one. Ed called it a miracle and even for him this was a wake-up call. He didn't believe in God and had had no intention of stopping drinking before that night. Sure, he knew things had got bad, but he was a player. Hell, if I could screw whoever I wanted, hang out with movie stars and spend whatever I liked whenever I liked without any worry at all of running out of cash, I'd drink and use like a lunatic too.

We met in Alcoholics Anonymous in 1995 and from the outset were firm buddies. It still seems pretty extraordinary that we met at all, given where he and I both came from, me a middle-class English guy from London, him a poor Italian American from New York, but such is life. His old man had a scrap yard that sold junk to anyone who could find a use for it. It had been a family business since his great-grandfather had emigrated from Italy back in the day with nothing but ambition, desperation and a family to feed. As a kid he and his brothers (he had a few – those fucking Catholics bred like bunnies in those days) would skip school and hang out in the yard exploring, learning sales patter from their dad, getting tanned and building muscles by shifting old car engines, bits of furniture and other things that any kid would just love to get their little hands dirty with.

Being Italian, in the scrap business, and in New York I can't help thinking they must have helped dispose of other more dodgy things but I don't care and don't want to know, which is why I've never asked him.

Ed was the first kid in his family to get into college. He put himself through it by working two jobs. One of those jobs was at a clothes store and he realised pretty quickly that he could do a hell of a lot better at dressing the local population than the old guy who owned the store; tweed had never been hip and in a university town it was downright suicidal. So Ed lied to the bank, falsified some paperwork and got a loan for his own shop. By twenty-two he was a millionaire. By twenty-five he was a millionaire tenfold, and by thirty he owned a hugely successful nationwide fashion retailer. It still wasn't enough for him so he moved to Europe and did the same thing there.

I guess he was lucky that he didn't drink it all away, but even Keith Richards would have a problem getting through that much cash.

I had shuffled into AA six months after Ed, having lost all my friends, most of my dignity and an awful lot of weight. I had spent the last few years drinking every day, snorting enormous amounts of speed and dropping acid on a daily basis. I was hearing voices, couldn't string a sentence together and was spiritually, morally and financially bankrupt. Thanks entirely to AA I have not taken a drink since 1995 and over the past twelve years beautiful, bald Ed has been my most consistent and valued friend.

According to him, I'm the only person he knows who has not asked him for money during the course of our decade-long friendship, which I imagine is one of the reasons we are so close.

It must also be said that, like so many self-made men, he is a real hard ass when it comes to business. A couple of years after we first met I was working in the City, chasing money in a desperate attempt to gain some kind of fulfilment, security and parental approval.

He would often call me at seven in the morning and the exchange would inevitably go something like this:

'Dude! What are you up to?' he'd shout down the phone.

'Eating breakfast – it's 7 a.m. and I just crawled out of bed. Please lower your voice.'

'Breakfast? You fucking bum! I've been in the office over an hour already – get your ass in the car and go to work, you fucking hippie!' with which he'd hang up. As it turned out I was a fucking bum for having lunch and dinner as well. But all this only endeared him to me further.

Ed has houses around the world; he drives Aston Martins and Porsches, fancies my wife and is godfather to my son. I've not once heard him moan or complain about life; he shows up for his kids and he recently got married to a Swedish girl thirty years younger than him to whom he's been faithful ever since they started dating. He comports himself with dignity and humility, and is for sure the most honourable man I've ever met. The Bible-toting hicks in Utah would no doubt say, 'Ah, but is he happy?' all ready to prove with glee the 'money can't buy you happiness' theory.

Well, fuck those assholes. Whoever said money can't buy you happiness clearly never had any. Hell, yeah, he's happy. And graceful with it. On my way to the Refuge, as he walked me to the security line at Heathrow he put his arms around me and said, 'Josh, there are three things you're going to need to survive this trip: surrender, willingness and money. As usual I'll take care of the easy one. You're going to have to do the other two. I'm proud of you, dude.' Then he hugged me and sent me on my way.

My first impression of the Refuge was that it would be a nice place to die in. It was clean, welcoming, friendly and warm. I walked through the doors into the nurses' station for my admission. I was wearing the woolly hat that had been on my head for almost every hour of the last six months, sunglasses even though it was 9 p.m. and pitch black outside, and a T-shirt and jeans that hadn't been washed for at least four months. It was as if my hat and glasses were my only protection against the world – if they were removed I was quite positive that I'd be exposed to terrible things and simply explode.

I also had an inability to touch door handles due to the risk of contamination, and my hands couldn't stop shaking.

I had thick bandages on each arm and I was so far beyond tired that I caught myself falling asleep every few minutes against my will. The only reason BA let me on the flight in the first place was because I was wearing a very expensive cashmere coat that hid my wounds, had dosed myself up on happy pills so I could sound coherent at check-in, and was flying business class.

The nurse took one look at me and paged the psychiatrist. I gathered that he was meant to see me in the morning but apparently the nurse didn't know if I would make it that long without some pretty strong meds. I dozed off while waiting for him to arrive. Apart from my brief but charming instructions to Ray, I had yet to utter a word.

Thirty minutes later a good-looking young guy in the obligatory white coat arrived. Dr Well (seriously) introduced himself to me and offered me a seat in his office. He spent a few minutes looking over the notes that had been faxed to him by my psychiatrist, again thanks to Ed, and then looked up at me.

'Well, Josh. Why do you think you're here?' he started.

I shrugged non-committally and broke eye contact.

'How much anxiety are you feeling right now, with one being fine and ten being the most anxious you could be?' he tried, pen hovering expectantly above his assessment pad.

I couldn't stop myself from sniggering.

'How about depression, using the same scale?'

He was nothing if not persistent.

I put my head in my hands and fell asleep again.

The next thing I felt was a pair of hands helping me up and leading me gently to a bedroom immediately next to the nurses' station. I'm given two orange pills (100mg of Seroquel, I found out later) and a larger white pill (my buddy clonazepam, or Klonopin as they call it in the US). I swallowed them and fell on to the small single bed fully clothed. All I felt was relief at being carried away into sleep, as far away from my physical body as possible.

The usual admission process at the Refuge involves the patient spending one or two nights in the 'acute care' ward by the nurses' station. They are then moved to a shared room with two other patients on the campus proper. The ward is comprised of five tiny rooms situated around a central nursing station.

Occasionally an addict during a particularly heavy detox will spend three nights in acute care and in extreme cases four nights are necessary.

I was kept there for seventeen nights.

My mental and physical states had been so depleted and I was considered so dangerous both to myself and possibly to others, that I was kept under twenty-four-hour observation for each of those eighteen days. I could not even take a shit without having a male nurse in the bathroom with me. The rule was that I had to be within arm's distance of a nurse every minute of every day whether eating, sleeping, showering or attending medical appointments. I challenge anyone to manage to take a dump while a large psychiatric nurse is sitting there watching you. I found out just how long the human body can go without getting rid of its accumulated waste (a magnificent eight days in my case, before I simply exploded with such relief that I wouldn't have cared if the Pope was watching).

On my third day Brad, the executive director of the Refuge, came to see me. He remembered Ed from twelve years previously and had kept in touch with him over the years. He told me that Ed had spoken with him and told him that I was to be kept there at his expense for as long as was necessary to recover and get well. Brad revealed that initially every member of the intake department had vetoed my admission. They all felt that I was too much of a liability to accept both from a legal and a medical stand-point. Thanks (yet again) to Ed and his influence (no doubt the threat of no more donations played a considerable part), Brad had overruled the decision and insisted I be allowed to come. He made it clear, however, that should I harm myself or anyone else there I would be immediately transferred to a federal psychiatric lockdown facility in Phoenix by the police.

A lockdown sounded quite appealing to me. I asked him if I could go there voluntarily, and if I would be allowed to smoke there. He looked at me, clearly a little disturbed that I was even considering it, and said, 'Josh, trust me,' you really don't want to end up there. You're basically chained to a bed sixteen hours a day in a room full of the state's most disturbed mental patients and kept heavily medicated. It would be very hard to get out again, believe me.' Again, I found it hard to see any negatives.

Later that day, I decided that in fact I really did prefer the idea of the lockdown to where I was. At least I wouldn't be required to do anything there. As I lay in my bed under the covers with my nurse sitting in a chair by the door, I unwrapped the razor blade I'd hidden in my toothpaste and removed easily enough earlier on, patting myself on the back for having had the foresight to come prepared. I took off the bandages and started to slice through the healing wounds on my arms again. It wasn't so hard this time, even without any ice, and before long I could feel warm, wet blood seeping through my fingers like gravy. I closed my eyes and waited.

Edison, my burly, black, one-to-one nurse was good at his job. He noticed the blood dripping to the floor pretty quickly and sounded the alarm. Sheets were ripped off, gloves were put on, bandages applied, and there was plenty of running around and talking urgently. I just lay there smiling, far, far beyond caring about the chaos I was creating.

The police were called and I was escorted to the nearest hospital to be properly treated. Brad called Ed as a courtesy to let him know there was nothing he could do but alert the authorities and have me transferred to the lockdown unit. Ed begged him to give me another chance. He called on his years of friendship, vast financial donations, and spent over an hour on the phone pitching, cajoling, threatening and pleading. After much persuasion Brad agreed to give me a twenty-four-hour reprieve. If I changed my attitude and complied with their policies I could stay. But it was made clear that there would be no more chances, and in fact Ed himself told Brad that if I continued to fuck around he had his blessing to do whatever he felt was appropriate.

I was moved back into the nurses' station and basically lay in bed heavily medicated and unconscious for eighteen hours a day. It was at least a week before I started to become a little more lucid. There was just enough of a break in the thick, black cloud of my depression to start conversing something like normally and on my tenth day I was told to go and see the psychologist.

I was led to another building – my first time outside the nurses' station – and followed my bodyguard into a comfortable-looking and welcoming complex. I could see cactuses and palm trees out of the window, and Edison led me up to a walnut-brown door with the name Dr Feinburg on it. He knocked and pushed the door open for me.

I'm sitting in a cool, air-conditioned office 5,000 miles from home with a bearded man who has nice eyes. The man, my new shrink Dr Feinburg, has read my file and he informs me quite nonchalantly that I have recently become 'orphanised' and then looks at me for my reaction. I simply stare at him through medicated eyes and try to disappear.

I am thirty years old, it's true that my father died a few years ago, but my mother is alive, happily widowed and, as far as I know, going about her life in the bustle of London with as much vigour as any other woman in her mid sixties. And yet I am, apparently, an orphan.

The truth is that I did have just about enough clarity to accept the fact that in all honesty I couldn't disagree with what he said. Over the past year the circumstances of my life have unquestionably severed all connection with my family – my mother, brother, grandparents, uncles and aunts: the whole damn tribe. And although it feels like I have had a limb amputated, there is a part of me that feels an enormous amount of relief. As if the leg that was cut off was gangrenous, weeping and smelling like a sewer, and to be rid of it, even without a decent prosthetic, has brought with it the possibility of an immediate end to the persistent and staggering level of self-hatred and disgust I have been carrying for so long.

After twenty minutes of talking largely to himself, Dr Feinburg told me to take some time to recover physically and that he would see me again in a few days. I was led back to my little room and slept for another fourteen hours.

After a fortnight of behaving myself I was allowed to start attending group therapy sessions. Luckily most of these were led by Dr Feinburg whom I actually grudgingly admired – he seemed wholly genuine and without the forced sterility of the other doctors I had come into contact with both there and at other institutions.

Everyone in my little group of six (my primary group, as it was known) had spent a good few days getting to know one another. There were three men (two sex addicts and me) and three women (co-dependent alcoholics all of them). As I entered the room with my bodyguard behind me, arms covered in bandages, my hat still on but minus the shades (seen as significant progress) they turned to stare. Word had been spreading about this weird British guy and I guess they were curious and perhaps a little nervous to meet me.

'All right everyone. Let's get started,' said Dr Feinburg.

We all took our seats in a small circle in the middle of the room.

'Everyone raise their right hand and let's take the pledge,' he continued. 'I swear that everything that is said and done in this room stays in this room. And that's for life.'

I raised my left hand and as everyone repeated it I mumbled nonsense – very schoolboyish, but no way was I going to go through with this without having the option of talking about it afterwards, even if it was with a bunch of stoned crazies in a lockdown unit.

'Now, as we have a new member, Josh, let's do introductions,' said the doc. He turned to me. 'Josh, when we have anyone new join us, we go around the room and state our claims, the reasons we're here, and allow you to start to get to know us. Once we've done that we can spend some time getting to know you. Brian, why don't you start and we'll go to your left.'

Brian turned to look at me. He was about forty-five and deeply unattractive – considerably overweight with pock-marked skin and greasy hair.

'Hi, Josh. I'm Brian. I'm here for sex addiction and alcoholism. Um, I'm in my second week and am focusing on self-esteem, boundaries and containment. My affirmation for today is "I am worth loving".'

I couldn't help laughing. Jesus Christ, I had sunk to the bottom of the fucking pit. I had no idea what he was talking about but I knew instantly that there was nothing remotely worth loving about that fat fuck.

Then a young girl of about twenty-one looked at me. She was quite pretty in an American, girl-next-door kind of way, with frizzy blonde hair and long legs. The Refuge had strict rules about revealing too much flesh, but I could tell she had decent tits and worked out regularly.

'Hi Josh. I'm Mandy. I'm here for alcoholism and co-dependency. I'm also in my second week and am working on my reality, my connection to my spirit and getting to know my inner child. My affirmation is "I am enough".'

Fuck me, this was an ordeal. The more we went around the room, the more anxious I became. I desperately wanted some fresh air and a cigarette and my legs, hands and head had started twitching.

Finally everyone had had their say: Brian, Mandy, Candice, Scott and Jennifer had all affirmed themselves, shared their pain and told me what aspects of their fragile lives they were working to better.

'Thanks, everyone,' said Dr Feinburg. 'Now, Josh. Why don't you tell us why you're here?'

Five pairs of eyes turned to look at me.

I was rooted to the spot. In the midst of my terror, I realised something that seemed important. Everything I had been doing with my life thus far was aimed at being invisible and unknowable. I could continue like that and end up dead or I could take a risk with these strangers and speak.

'Go fuck yourself,' I said to Dr Feinburg. Pretty pithy, I thought.

There was an excited murmur and Dr Feinburg did what any self-respecting shrink would do. He gave me the 'empathy nod' and continued to stare at me.

I'm sure they teach that nod at medical school. More than a tip, less than a bow, just the right side of vigorous but always supportive and understanding. The 'I'm listening to you and understanding you in a safe and contained way' nod.

'We have a good couple of hours, Josh. And I know that everyone, myself included, wants to get to know you. Why don't you start by telling us where you're from?' he suggested.

'Read the file – it's all there, dude,' I countered.

'I have read the file, but I'm not allowed to reveal its contents to anyone else here. And I think that would be a shame. I think if you took a risk and talked to us now you might experience something rather special,' he said.

There was a long silence while my brain whirled furiously around trying to see all the angles, the pros and cons, traps and pitfalls, benefits and disadvantages. Were there hidden cameras here? Were these guys actors? Police? Should I leave? Was I strong enough to drop Edison and make it out of the campus?

In the end my brain just shuddered to a halt. I literally was incapable of thinking any more. Like in those movies where they shoot the bad guy up with a truth serum and he gives up the will to resist any more.

'Ah, fuck it then. If you want to hear my story I'll tell it to you. It's not particularly interesting but it seems like there's nothing else to do this afternoon,' I said in a rare moment of surrender. 'Just remember you asked me to do this, so if you get bored, tough shit.'

I closed my eyes and took myself back to the very beginning. Always a good place to start.

My favourite book is Paul Auster's *Mr Vertigo* – if you can spare the cash, it's well worth a punt. It opens with the line: 'I was twelve years old the first time I walked on water.' Well, you know what? Fuck him – I was three years old the first time I learned how to *fly* and I know which one I'd rather be able to do. Up until today, I think it saved my life.

Now I'm thirty, I want to die but I seem incapable of making that happen. Suicide seems to be getting a bad press these days but it strikes me that far from being the easy way out, sometimes suicide is genuinely the only possible solution. Perhaps by the end of this you will agree with me.

1979-80

Memory is a funny thing. It seems that life's best experiences are often forgotten within days or hours of the event and that the incidents that hurt the most live on in us until the day we die.

As a three-year-old, my memories were just starting to be formed and retained. One of the first things I remember as clear as day is the look of irritation on my father's face as he removed my nappy and saw that I was wet. He liked his little boy clean and dry, thank you very much. Out came the baby wipes and it was a few minutes until he felt I was clean enough for his needs. He gave me a drink of something that tasted disgusting (red wine, I think) and sighed with either impatience or lust (I find it hard to tell the difference even as an adult) until I was drowsy and pliable, then he lowered his head to my cock and spent ten minutes down there blowing me. I think this might be one of the reasons I continued to wear nappies until I was five – anything to try to put him off me during those night-time visits. Hey, you do the best you can with what you've got, which unfortunately ain't a lot when you're tiny, alone and naked with a giant. My father was 220 pounds, 6 feet 5 inches and an immense, impenetrable oak tree of a man. I was 3 feet tall, barely 40 pounds and felt like a pebble to his mountain.

The most disgusting thing to me was his saliva, his craggy, hot mouth and pockmarked tongue slathering reams of stringy, sticky spit all over me – my stomach, legs, thighs, shoulders. Despite my body's reaction ('You see you like it, you're hard') and the occasional shameful thrill of physical pleasure, this feeling of being licked, stained, will disgust and haunt me to this day. I imagine him seeping through my pores, a sickening osmosis, into my bloodstream and to the very root of me, residing like a thickening black sludge there for ever. This is the material inside me that actually makes me bad. I know that there is no way of getting rid of it. Once it is there it solidifies and moulds itself around my insides, becoming a concrete waste-ground, anchored to my soul and permanent.

And fuck you if you're thinking, Honestly, how disgusting to talk about things like that. I don't want to hear that kind of filth. Don't fucking listen then. Piss off back to your room, put Beyoncé on the stereo and go back to your world of petty resentments, gossip and ennui. This is *my* story, and I'll tell it the way it is.

Ha! Score one for the untold millions of shaking little boys and girls hidden behind the false safety of Daddy's nice job and charitable donations and their big comfortable bedrooms adorned with soft bears who can only stare through their blind, black, beady eyes at the atrocities going on each night.

Jesus Christ, his balls were enormous – they scared the shit out of me, this freckled globe of wrinkles and hair drooping and swinging in front of my face, his hand blurring above them in fast forward until I knew he was soon about to leave. And what a fucking mess afterwards. Too much for my mouth, too uncontrollable to direct safely in any one place, it would spew forth into my hair, over my Noah's Ark bedspread, up the walls. And it was hot! Even at three I knew this was weird. Not quite right. More stains to carry around no matter how hard I scrubbed.

By the time he left my room, I felt like a sack of dirty rags he had been rummaging around in – scraps of worthless trash covered in shit.

Learning how to fly is surely the reason I am still here twenty-seven years later (albeit maybe not for much longer). After a few such experiences with my father I remember the exact second when I said to myself (or was it God finally sparing an angel for a few precious seconds?), 'Let him do whatever he wants to me. I'm not going to fight it,' and as if a switch had been flicked somewhere up high, I immediately flew out of the room. This was some deal, believe me. I was flying. Totally free, with no idea as to the guilt lurking patiently that would dominate me as I grew up and remembered surrendering to him and not fighting back. I'd fly out of my body, down the corridor, over the banister and a gentle landing on the bristly front door mat. The scratchiness on my back felt somehow reassuring. I *was* still alive. And I was liberated.

The relief was short-lived. Within a few seconds the bats would come. Dozens of the little fuckers, dive-bombing me like demented Messerschmitt pilots shrieking over Westminster, blinded by the thrill of taking lives. Pecking, biting, invading; taking their time and savouring the immobile, warm young flesh offered to them, just like the monster in my room.

This happened every time he'd come for me from then on. I got to fly at least three times a week and didn't even care about the bats after a while. I learned early on that there is never anything genuinely good in this world without a decent helping of shit to counterbalance it. Boo fucking hoo.

From the age of three or four I became (quite despite my best intentions) a manipulative, conniving, two-faced, controlling, disgusting beast. It seemed to happen as slowly and as naturally as a tumour growing in an old man's lung. Like watching the hour hand of a clock, I only noticed something had changed further down the line. At times I was, at least on the outside, charming, funny and seemingly even altruistic as a child and as a young man. But deep in my cave the Gollum inside me was sneering and growing. Learning to adapt and survive in the only way he knew how. You get what you want through stealth and cunning and God help you if you take your eye off the ball for even a second.

I would lie in my bed, listening to cars driving by outside and feel both reassured and appalled that there was actually a world outside far away from this, where these things didn't happen. Reassured that if I controlled things just so, behaved just right, just maybe, eventually, I could end up there. Appalled that a world could carry on as normal outside when these things were happening to me that made me feel so unhappy and alone.

Ironically I never once even imagined that anything was seriously untoward in my life. This was it: childhood was an assault course of terror and dread that had to be survived by any means necessary. And nature in her infinite capacity for survival had given me everything I needed to get through each day, including the cruel, childish hope that I could somehow in the future escape to something better.

The body and mind's innate ability to endure is astonishing. Like swimming in a pool of ping-pong balls, the more I pushed what was happening to me down, the more weird stuff came up to the surface. First came the tic – a vocal twitch that sounded like a frog on helium. It would arrive suddenly, completely unannounced and force its way through my body and out of my mouth never once asking permission. And if it didn't come out right the first time it would have to be immediately repeated four or five or six times until the timbre was just right. It made reading out loud in class a total liability. It served its purpose by forcing me to shut the fuck up and speak only when absolutely necessary. An important early lesson for me: if you're silent people don't notice you and the chances of bad things happening are therefore significantly reduced. Shut up, head down, tread silently and carefully.

Next came the nightmares: running away from faceless monsters to find my legs turning slowly to stone, my tiny (always naked) body sweating and straining against my immobile legs, willing them to move before I got caught. They never did and the nightmares continue to this day. I've been stabbed, shot, set on fire, raped, stoned, beaten, eaten alive, drowned, humiliated and hacked to pieces a thousand times by mobs of angry men and would awaken shocked, with tears mingling with the sweat on my pillow, breathing in short desperate gasps.

While still at nursery school I would get a perverse thrill from fantasising about being held down and tortured and begging for my life. Something about actually saying the words, 'Please stop. I'll do anything if only you'll stop,' made me feel more powerful than just shutting up and taking cock. Perhaps someone stronger would have actually said those things for real. Would it have made a difference if I had found that voice?

Around the same time as the nightmares started, I developed something the experts call 'magical thinking'. What a great expression. I couldn't cross the road until I had seen a red car, otherwise someone would die. Cracks on the pavement were to be avoided at all costs. The light switch in my bedroom had to be flicked on and off exactly six times in a precise rhythm, followed by a run and a jump at least four feet away from the bed to avoid the monsters hiding underneath. Once in bed the duvet would have to be wrapped firmly around my body like a human sausage roll, arms straight down by my sides, eyes staring at the ceiling too afraid to be closed, calves taut with terror. Counting objects and simply reciting sequences of numbers became an addiction. The beauty and mystery of numbers was a great distraction and even now if I see a telephone number once it is memorised instantly. And don't get me started on the sheer beauty and seduction and comfort of prime numbers – one of the truly great mysteries of the universe.

My every action seemed to be dominated by mythical suspicions that were all too real to me, but whose rules would constantly change all by themselves, so just as I would get used to acting in a certain way (counting only blue cars, for example), the colour would change to yellow cars and God help me if I missed one. Precise rhythms needed to be tapped out with fingers or ticked vocally before speaking, moving, sometimes even before breathing. I just knew there was an almighty and omnipotent being watching me at all times just waiting for me to fuck up and mete out the appropriate punishment. I existed in a state of high alert, senses honed to a level MI5 would be proud of. I think the shrinks call it hypervigilance. Any kind of sudden noise and I would literally jump two feet in the air.

My fear of contamination started around this time too, I think because I felt so stained and dirty after what my father had done to me. If anyone breathed on me or touched me, or even if I was to touch something that someone else had come into contact with, I would feel that shame and filth all over again. Hands needed to be washed after contact with door handles or anything that others' might have touched and I would use the sleeve of my coat or jumper to open doors, stand as far away from people as I could when they were talking to me, and flinch at anyone's touch.

The stomach problems followed soon afterwards. Every morning without fail I would run into the bathroom for my twenty minutes in the toilet (a few precious moments of safety behind a blessedly locked door) and it would inevitably be an ordeal only those on a cheap gap year in India could compete with. Blasting shit into the bowl, my stomach cramping, sweat pouring off me, nauseous and light-headed, trying to ignore the blood on the toilet paper. Occasionally fighting the need to bury my head in the loo afterwards and shake it around in my own waste, screaming into the filth that was a part of me. At night, too, I would invariably need to go to the loo again. This time I would sit there trying to be as quiet as possible even though the upstairs bathroom had a heavy, creaking door with a lock that sounded like a gunshot. I would carefully push the door to, but more often than not my slumbering giant of a father would awaken and tramp to the bathroom, sitting quietly beside me as I finished and insisting on wiping me – making sure I was 'nice and clean'. He told me he enjoyed it and explained that that was what fathers were for. It didn't matter that his stubby fingers would often break through the thin piece of tissue and have a good feel around while I sat there staring silently at my feet which didn't even touch the carpet yet. 'Honestly, Dad, it's fine. I can do it myself,' I would plead in what was a pathetic and feeble way of telling him to stop. But of course I was ignored entirely as he carried on oblivious.

At four and a half this all seemed a bit too overwhelming for me. I think that the vast reserves of energy needed for day-to-day living had been exhausted. I was desperate for a way out. One Saturday afternoon, my mother had invited some of her friends round for afternoon tea. It was something she used to do occasionally; she loved a good gossip and was a very depressed and competitive woman. Having company allowed her to check how well or badly other families were doing, slag off her enemies and compare notes on everyone else's life.

As they sat laughing and chatting in the living room, I sneaked into the kitchen and found a carving knife in one of the big drawers. I wasn't really sure what I was doing – I was going more on instinct alone. Sharp things were dangerous. My throat was soft. Therefore putting one into the other should result in death and an end to the pain. Made sense to me.

As my mother came into the kitchen for more pastries or teabags or whatever the fuck she thought her guests wanted she saw me huddled behind the table trying to find the correct entry position for the knife. There ensued a brief chase around the table before she overpowered me, dragged me into the living room and told everyone what I had just done. She told it with a certain amount of glee, like she actually wanted to humiliate me, to show me up for being a weak, overly dramatic asshole. I remember thinking how cruel this was – it shouldn't be happening like this. Their laughter (hers the loudest) stays with me today. Of course I was ashamed but more than that was a feeling of confusion: I wasn't aware that I had been doing anything wrong. Why were they laughing at me? Why did she even stop me? If I didn't exist any more then they could carry on their lives unburdened and free of me. It seemed like a good deal for all of us. I was so sick and so tired. I felt so damn old already.

1981

I began to learn the art of invisibility. At five I started going to primary school, and like a whoring, guilty Harry Potter, I would put on my invisibility cloak as I arrived, praying that I could simply keep my head down and avoid attention. I marvelled at the other kids sharing jokes or hanging out in the playground. I became intimately familiar with the locked inside of the toilet cubicles, my trusty TARDIS of safety, however temporary. Somehow everyone except me had been given instructions on how to act in social situations. I couldn't even ask another boy to pass the juice at lunch I was so terrified.

I had an elder brother, Max, who went to the same school. He and I had despised each other for as long as I had been alive. I have no idea if my father was doing to him what he was doing to me, in fact I was pretty sure that he wasn't, and I was convinced that my dad loved Max much more than me. Max was the good son – bright, athletic and popular. We both seemed to be in intense competition with one another for our parents' love and attention and for that reason we hated one another passionately. Every break-time at school we would kick the shit out of each other in the playground. It happened so often that it became almost part of the school timetable and scores of other kids would gather around to watch while the teachers stood at the back pretending not to notice anything untoward, in magnificent 1980s style.

Max was to grow up very much in our father's image: a fine-wine-drinking, Oxbridge-educated accountant who went to the ballet and professed a great love of cricket. I saw him as a fraud, nothing more than a charlatan who drank too much and settled for the life he felt he should live rather than the one he really wanted to. I hated the fact that everything that was his got passed on to me: not only his clothes and toys but now also his education.

I longed to have the fraternal relationship that I witnessed in other brothers at school – protective, sharing, loving – but nothing could be further from the reality of our relationship. We seemed to be arch-enemies, predestined since birth to hate and abhor one another. Over time we learned simply to tolerate each other as adults. A part of me wishes we could sit down together, maybe with a therapist, and talk about things but I'm scared about what we would find. I can't ever imagine him speaking honestly (there are certain parts of his private life I have learned about that I find pretty unspeakable), and truthfully I just don't like the guy. The hatred that children can feel seems purer and more violent than that felt by adults, at least in my experience, and it would take something of a miracle to put such a sadistic and vicious past behind us.

I had my first orgasm during that term (my father was not what you would call a considerate sexual partner). During one of the gym classes (God, the unimaginable horror of changing in front of the other boys) we were taught how to climb ropes. I got about halfway up and experienced the most pleasurable and entirely new sensation as my cock rubbed against the thick twine. A feeling of calm came over me, a release and sense of relaxation from the unmitigated stress of my miniature life. This rapidly became the high spot of my week and such was my excitement and immersion in this new joy I didn't even notice the curious stares of the gym teacher as I took just that little bit longer than the others to finish on the ropes.

Mr Sperring was a balding, older man. Stocky and solid with the detachment that all gym teachers seem to have, he was not a *proper* teacher and he knew it. No curriculum to adhere to, no exams to worry about or papers to mark. Not even really answerable to the head. Just a guy who made little boys run around in their tiny shorts, working up a sweat for a few hours a week. And for some inexplicable reason, he seemed to like me.

He grabbed me one afternoon in the short break before lunch and led me excitedly into the equipment room off the main gym hall. The room was small and filled with gym mats, medicine balls and stacked chairs but there was a small table and desk where he did what little paperwork was needed. He shut the door and asked me if I wanted a present. I was busy trying to figure out if this was a trap or not and didn't answer. He reached into his pocket and pulled out a small Swiss army knife – it was tiny, like out of a Christmas cracker, and was by far the coolest thing I had ever seen. Then just like that he gave it to me. Told me not to show it to anyone and definitely not to say where I got it from otherwise he'd be in serious trouble. He was trusting me, he said. He let me go to lunch then and I ate one-handed with my little paw stuffed deep in my pocket holding my new treasure, so excited I could hardly breathe.

The next couple of gym classes were strange: Mr Sperring completely ignored me, and stupid, friendless fool that I was I became quite desperate to get his attention. I would run as fast as I could and try to catch his eye and smile. My eyes asking the question and showing my confusion. It worked. The next day he caught me coming down the stairs by the gym and took me to his special room again. This time I got a box of matches. I could barely contain my excitement at being treated in such an adult way. I felt a part of me leave that invisible cloak and step into a new skin. I felt daring and emboldened. The bleak memories of the previous night's sticky horrors receded and the pain in my tummy eased off. I had a friend. And I was pathetically grateful. Like a mangled stray with a gammy leg given a bowl of water by a stranger. There was for the first time a feeling of excitement at the future. There was the potential for good to happen.

Half-term was a relentless frenzy of my put-upon, depressed mother literally dragging me around the park, forcing pizza down me in the zoo café and rushing me back home so she could lie in bed sobbing and treating her frequent migraines. The night visits occurred with dreadful regularity and the days seemed just too long. My mother had the bizarre need to be constantly close to me yet at the same time she was totally unable to see me. Our relationship until I was in my twenties was one where she would insist on almost hourly contact with me and yet she was genuinely incapable of hearing anything I said. There was a constant frantic dialogue in her head at all times, some of which she verbalised, some of which she kept to herself, but the result was that she existed only in her world and was utterly unreachable by anyone else.

She was, is, a deeply unhappy woman. One of those people for whom nothing is ever right. It is too warm or too cold; too loud or too quiet; too cheap or too expensive. We would get into the car to go somewhere for lunch and it would start: 'We should have left ages ago, we're bound to be late . . . The traffic will be terrible . . . Oh God, why does every light have to be red . . . I think the whole of London has gone completely mad – look at how they're driving . . . We should have got the bus, we'll never be able to park . . . I don't even know why we're going anyway, the food will be awful. . . I don't have any change for the meter, we'll have to stop . . . I'm bound to get a ticket . . . Jesus, it is so busy in town; why is everyone here? We should have gone a different way, I wonder if it's too late to change course . . . Oh shit, the road's up. That's it, we're never going to make it, what a disaster, I bet everyone else will be there on time . . . and I never should have worn this outfit . . . my hair is a total mess.'

You get the idea.

What's strange is that she was and is a very intelligent, capable woman. She can deal with a thousand thoughts going through her head at once, makes quick decisions based on sound evaluation, is generous, and capable of great compassion. Now, after many years of therapy, she has mellowed somewhat. She's my mum, and I can say that I love her today. During my childhood, though, she was distraught, depressed (needing hospitalisation at times) and unmedicated, save for Valium, which did not seem to make the slightest difference except to ensure that she slept through the night oblivious to the noises coming from my bedroom. She was denied a proper education by her parents, married very young to a narcissistic paedophile, had no life experience and yet was supposed to raise a family, keep a home and find fulfilment all by herself. Christ, no wonder the woman was in trouble. I think she felt that having kids would provide some answers; when I was in my early twenties she told me that my brother and I were desperate attempts to fix an already toxic marriage. It clearly didn't work.

I craved intimacy with her and yet could never find it. I would act in the way I thought she wanted but inevitably she would find fault with me just as she would with everything else. As a young child I would sit alone in her bath trying on her face creams and finding such comfort in smelling of her. As a teenager I would masturbate incessantly, thinking about her, desperate for a close intimate connection, if only in my head. I think to be fair to her that she wanted the same thing but had no idea how to manufacture it.

When I was a young child, she would often walk around naked and I couldn't take my eyes off her white little tits. She would leave her used panties lying around, which I would happen upon. I'd see the pale yellow, still moist stains in them and be secretly thrilled that she had been aroused at some point that day.

Unfortunately, it seemed that one of the few ways she had of connecting with me was by humiliating me: cruel comments in front of others, pointed remarks about my inadequate body (fat legs, balls too big and so on), jokes about sex that mortified me.

I'll never forget one evening after dinner when I was about eight. Dad had rented a video for us all to watch but either hadn't checked the certificate or didn't care, because it was immediately apparent that it was unsuitable for kids – lashings of graphic sex and violence. In one scene early on in the film some guy was lying on top of a woman and they were kissing. He started to work his way down her body and the camera stayed on the woman's face as he obviously started going down on her. My mum just started laughing and said, 'Ah, I bet Josh doesn't even know what he's doing to her, do you, Josh? Do you know what they're doing?'

I was so ashamed; my father and brother were smirking, and my mum was just laughing. Sadly, even though my dad had been doing the same thing to me for years, I didn't make the connection. It never occurred to me that a man and a woman could do something like that for pleasure when for me it was so excruciating, and she definitely seemed to be enjoying it. So I just blushed and said, 'Sure I do. He's tickling her feet.' They all just started howling then.

Half-term was an ordeal.

I returned to school wondering what I would receive next from my only friend in his musty warm grotto. I had even dared to dream that he could take me away from home and let me live with him. What kid knows about custody, court orders and the legalities of something like that?

My heart was thudding one break-time as he led me into the gym and across the room to our special place on my fourth day back at school. This time I was so excited I barely noticed that he locked the door and I looked on the table to see what he had for me. It looked like a magazine and I could scarcely contain my disappointment. It was too big to hide and looked creased and worn. Mr Sperring was acting differently too – his breathing was heavier and there was an urgency to his movements. He told me to open the magazine and look at it. There were dozens of pictures of naked women with enormous tits and vile hairy things between their legs. The photos were entirely unlike the few glimpses I'd seen of my mother's neat and tidy little cunt. These were rubbery, burgundy-coloured wounds surrounded by thick matted hair.

The shock of it hit me like a bucket of icy cold water. I didn't even notice how close behind me he was until I felt his warm breath in my ear and sensed him looking over my shoulder, crouching down behind me. In one quick movement he pulled down my trousers and turned me to face him. His hands grabbed my skinny hips and the familiar wetness surrounded me around my groin. I didn't say a word. I was too baffled. Even when he turned me round and started licking me somewhere very wrong I didn't say anything. I just held on to the table, my cheek resting on the cool wood and tried to fly away. This time the angels were too busy. I couldn't escape. The pain of his fingers inside me (I assumed that's what it was) stopped me taking off and I felt the walls slam down inside me. I'd obviously done something terribly wrong. I was so sorry I had made him angry. Once again I had committed some crime without being aware of it, and I felt myself blushing with the shame of having screwed up again. How could I be better if I didn't know what I was doing wrong? This time I felt his stuff spurt on to my ass and run down my legs. It was hotter than my dad's and there seemed to be more of it.

He told me afterwards that I had made him do this to me. I was too beautiful for my own good, he said. He told me that I was so sexy it was a sin. If I told anyone about it then I would be the one who got in trouble for doing something so disgusting. Thoughtfully, he informed me that he would protect me by not telling anyone as long as I was a good boy and did what he wanted me to do. Made sense to me. At least I had something he wanted. There was something about me that was special and worthy of desire. He even smiled at me and ruffled my hair as we said goodbye.

I tried to smile back, and said, 'Goodbye, Mr Sperring, sir.'

Years later I would find out that he was using an assumed name when he worked at the school, and would drive sixty miles every day to get to school and see his little boys. He was a ghost; a man who didn't exist and could vanish with impunity whenever he wanted to.

1982-6

The next five years were sickeningly repetitive. There was nowhere safe. Sleep was filled with nightmares and regular rude awakenings from my father who had added some new tricks to his routine. Maybe his moral compass had finally given out on him and he reckoned that there were no seedier depths to which he could plunge. I didn't matter to him any more as anything other than a toy.

I find it heartbreaking today, the extent to which I would go to think up ways to gain his approval. Each morning I'd lay the table for breakfast, making sure Dad's knife and fork were arranged the opposite way to ours because he was left-handed. I was never told to do this, I came up with it all on my own. He never acknowledged it and I felt even more ashamed for wanting him to love me so badly that I would rack my brains to think of new ploys. Somehow only a child could imagine a little thing like that could ever work. But it didn't stop me – whatever money I managed to accumulate I would save and spend on buying presents for him: wallets, cigars, chocolates. All to no avail.

Every day I would sink a little deeper into my dark cave, using it like a safety blanket to coddle me and warm me. I spent as much time as I could on my own or silently staring at the TV after dinner with my parents – a postcard of decent middle-class family life. I had become cripplingly shy to the point where I could not go to other kids' parties or any kind of social occasion, without being dismissed as rude because I wouldn't speak to anyone, and wandering around like a zombie.

Years later my wife would refer to it as 'Josh world': a self-protective state of dissociation and denial that came over me automatically at the slightest hint of danger. A simple question from my wife about what I wanted for dinner would instinctively result in me asking, 'Why?' followed by the barriers coming up and my mind going grey and blank. It was a bit like a car airbag going off immediately the car senses a crash; my mind was so honed and so constantly alert to threats that it would have to shut down at the slightest feeling that something was not quite right. So any question, anything unexpected or any kind of attention focused on me directly would result in the walls going up. The scariest thing to me was that it was utterly beyond my control. The alternative of being present and open was absolutely out of the question. When I was in Josh world, no matter how weird it seemed to others, I felt safe and protected – like the kid who shuts their eyes and believes that no one can see them.

One summer's holiday when I was about nine, we all went to the South of France. On the second day there we met in the hotel lobby to go to the beach, and I had forgotten my towel. My parents sent me back up to the room to get it and told me they'd wait for me. I was very much in Josh world that day, and it was only two hours later after the police had been called that they found me wandering around the hotel, completely oblivious to the fact that they had all been waiting for me, had paged me a dozen times over the intercom system, and had had the entire hotel staff searching for me. I had evidently started heading up to the room and simply got distracted and wandered off. I wasn't trying to be naughty or difficult, I was just like an automaton who had been pointed in one direction and carried on going.

By this stage in my life, Mr Sperring had given up any pretence at friendship or care. It was simple oral and anal rape on a regular basis. I was a dream date for a guy who liked to fuck children: beautiful, pliable, isolated, vulnerable, hidden and eager to please in any way I could. I know that a lot of paedophiles get off on the innocence of children; they really believe that they have fallen in love, that it is a natural and beautiful thing, an actual relationship. But I had lost all innocence. I was more attractive to a different kind of paedophile: the kind who simply wanted to use and abuse children. To inflict maximum pain and get off on the power and control they had over me. The kind of person who would give anything to have an eight-year-old boy in a soundproofed room with a bed, some rope and an assortment of 'toys' to use on him.

Ironically it was through my powerlessness that I came to understand that I had some kind of power over certain men. I became adept at flirting and manipulating them to get what I wanted, mainly attention. I gave off signals that would cause total strangers to stare at me transfixed, follow me into restaurant toilets, crave my company. My dream was to become a rent boy, conning clients into believing they were the ones in charge while actually using them and taking anything I could from them. At nine I was convinced I was gay and had found something I was actually good at. My body and sexuality were simply tools to be used to achieve attention and perhaps even love.

Of course no amount of attention was ever enough for me. What I really wanted was unconditional love and a feeling of safety, but I was just too damaged to get that from anyone by that stage. I'm also not even gay; I had just assumed that having sex with men was what people like me did.

At the same age, still hung up on the power thing, I would have these incredibly potent sexual fantasies about being the only survivor of a nuclear war (it was a realistic threat back then), and wandering around the streets pulling dead women out of cars and fucking them. When most kids were getting excited by the *A-Team*, I was trying to figure out how long dead bodies were still fuckable for.

1986-9

I decided at ten that I had to leave the school. I had been on automatic pilot for so long, cloaked in my grey fuzzy world, that I was shocked when the thought of moving schools popped into my mind. It was something of a eureka moment for me. I asked my parents if I could go to a boarding school. It would get me away from my depressed and neurotic mother and leave my father having to find an alternative outlet for his addictive, painful games, at least during term-time. Mr Sperring had by then moved on to new young flesh and to him I was now damaged goods.

To my relief my parents agreed with barely a thought, so I started at a boarding school in Yorkshire with a feeling of both reprieve at my escape and utter terror at the unknown. I was operating at such a level of anxiety that on the first day I threw up all the way there and my stomach was so bad, the pain so intense, that I was convinced I had appendicitis. I arrived, sweating, shaking, white as a sheet and petrified. As bad as my home life was, at least it was familiar. This new school was a blank canvas and I knew that it was going to hurt – out of the frying pan . . .

My stomach problems were so severe by now that pretty much every night I would spend an hour or more in the toilets some time around midnight, doubled over in agony. I wasn't sleeping, was barely eating and my concentration had diminished considerably. The headmaster took an instant dislike to me and the kids made me feel like an outsider who had dared to enter their world of cliques, clubs and indefinable rules.

Looking back, how I wish I could have been strong. Able to throw a punch, lash out, look after myself. But I'd taken shit for so long, had been powerless for so long, that I would just stand there silently taking whatever they threw at me. I don't think it ever occurred to me that I could fight back with fists, or even find some core of inner strength that would see me through relatively unscathed.

The only weapon I had at my disposal was my body. I threw myself at whoever would take me (not hard in an all-boys school) and spent hours locked in the loo with older boys, teachers, peers, anyone. This was my solace, my protection, my uniqueness. I figure that by thirteen I had had sexual relationships with over thirty other guys and counting.

I had never felt so alone and so miserable and yet thinking about my poor anxious mother at home I would write her three letters a day telling her how happy I was and how fabulous this school was. It seemed I could work hard at protecting her, just not myself. Occasionally when the pretence was simply too much I would hint that perhaps things weren't so rosy. The following day I would receive a teary phone call from her telling me that she had been up all night sobbing and worrying about me and was it her fault I was unhappy? She would urge me to be with people all the time, telling me never, ever to be on my own, that she was worried sick about me and had been getting terrible headaches as a result. I felt so awful at having made her feel this way that I would retreat back into my hole, reassuring her that actually everything was great and that I had loads of friends and was busy all the time.

I have never in my life had an honest conversation with my mother. I remember as a young teenager seeing an American soap on TV one day where the son would be chatting with his mother in their kitchen about his problems at school and his worries about girls or bullies or whatever and I was completely astonished. I couldn't imagine why the producers had allowed something so blatantly beyond the realms of possibility to be aired. Any kind of honesty with another human being, or even with myself for that matter, was anathema to me.

I would receive a letter from my father every fortnight, typed, often signed with his full name and without exception urging me to work hard, succeed academically and improve my grammar. He would go to great lengths to point out any errors in my letters to him. I was clearly baffled by the subtleties of 'who' and 'whom'. Once I accidentally split an infinitive and got three pages of notes on why this was the cardinal sin of the grammatical world. He was evidently very anxious that I might not succeed at school; he made me send him a weekly list of grades for each of my subjects and insisted that I got a minimum of all Bs. He made constant helpful suggestions that I should ask for more homework, ask for private tuition in the subjects I was struggling with (although I wasn't aware of struggling with any of them), and asked me to send him copies of my essays for his input and comments. I was ten years old, and not once in the three years I was at that school did he ask about my friends (or lack thereof), my state of mind, or tell me that he loved me.

I see now that my father (an eminent accountant and highly respected) could only try to guide me down the path that he was led as a child. I have no idea what happened to him as a kid nor do I care (though God knows his family is pretty fucked up), but I know beyond doubt that he believed everything he had done to me and continued to do to me was right. Even fucking his son was, I believe, to him a gesture of love and the right thing to do. This is the great truth of the narcissist: there is genuinely no other way but theirs, and trying to get them to see differently is like trying to break down a concrete wall with a toothpick.

Years later over a rare cup of coffee, a few months before he died from a massive coronary, he said to me that he had read in the papers the previous day about a guy who had been caught by the police with his penis in a ten-year-old girl's mouth. He chortled and said, 'Lucky sod!' I still remember that look in his eyes as he said it. Manic, lustful, crazed. Even if I wanted to, I don't think I could ever understand a man like that. I've not regretted his death once.

Two things happened that first term at boarding school that gave me real hope for the first time in my life. I started smoking in earnest and I started to study the cello. Years earlier at the age of four I remember having my first cigarette while visiting my father's mother, an elderly and utterly crazy woman with a priceless collection of rare books in her Belgravia apartment. She was a German immigrant who had married well when she came to London and was eccentric in the extreme. My mother hated her vehemently, and would constantly bitch about her to us. During this particular visit she taught me the art of smoking properly – inhaling and all. My parents laughed as she showed me how to light a cigarette and how to smoke it without getting the end wet. My coughing fits just provoked more laughter, and I look back and wonder what the fuck my parents (both of whom had never smoked in their lives) were doing. Despite the coughing fits and the taste, something about it, the magic of it all, got to me.

Smoking has remained for me one of the truly great pleasures in life. I like to call them my little hugs – each cigarette provides a deep sense of purpose and safety. Although I would smoke at my grandmother's house from the age of four, I didn't begin seriously until that first term at boarding school when I was ten. While most of the other kids were off playing football, I would be hidden in the trees puffing away furiously with my smokes for company.

I don't mean to harp on about it, especially as these days the world seems so anti-smoking, but for me smoking must make the shortlist of the world's greatest inventions. The excitement of getting a whole packet in its clean cellophane wrapper from the dodgy corner shop owner and stumbling into the woods, hands shaking to strike the match and take that first magical puff. The aloneness and sanctity of being hidden, often in the dark or rain with my new friend Marlboro was the greatest gift I had. I was to smoke faithfully as much and as often as I could for years to come. It was comforting to have a secret that wasn't disgusting or shaming. Something that I knew was illegal and that I wasn't supposed to be doing, but only I knew about it; it was my decision and a delicious secret just for me.

The cello was something different entirely. My teacher was a mediocre (at best) player but he gave me enough exercises to ensure I could lock myself in a practice room at every available moment and work on the symmetric, perfect magic of those four strings. Shite Lloyd Webber songs sounded utterly magnificent to me. Little sonatas by Vivaldi or Gabrielli fitted together flawlessly and my ears and mind could achieve a sense of perfect balance I had never felt before. My tic disappeared when playing, my stomach relaxed, my mind emptied, time stood still and I think I experienced real peace for the very first time.

I was good, too. Within a year I would often have other teachers walking into the practice room where I was working, expecting to find my cello teacher there and very surprised instead to see an eleven-year-old playing away furiously.

With music and cigarettes the bullying didn't matter. The night-time rapes, sometimes invited to ease the loneliness, more often endured passively and silently, became acceptable moments in time because I knew I had my escapes. When it got too much for me and the cello was unavailable I would steal off into the woods looking for small animals to kill.

Magnifying glasses trained on ants and daddy-long-legs would have literally explosive effects (even more fun when the legs are removed first). Newts and fish could be spliced perfectly in half with a well-aimed rock. There was no anger there and no sense of remorse, just a curious fascination at how deeply unimportant life is. Looking back, I can easily feel like a serial killer in the making. I was entirely separated from the world around me and no one seemed either to notice or to care.

1989–94

By the time I left that school at thirteen I was no longer being abused by my father. I was far too old for people like him. My identity had hardened into a fully formed, completely insular and self-sufficient machine. I started boarding at a middle-ranking but ludicrously expensive boys-only public school and immediately established my credentials as a piece of ass (charging the occasional Mars Bar or packet of smokes for the privilege). I continued to improve my cello playing and also discovered another one of life's miracles: alcohol.

The feeling of freedom and lightness caused by a half-bottle of vodka was the closest I came to flying again. The hospital admissions, suspensions, stomach pumps, arrests and headaches were a very small price to pay for feeling so invincible and complete.

I'll never forget the first time I got really drunk at thirteen. Walking down the stairs where each step seemed thirty feet tall and deciding instead just to fall down to save the effort, getting beaten senseless by the older boys because I couldn't feel any pain, coming to and finding one of the obese prefects going down on me, throwing up again and again. God, I loved it. The first time I dropped acid a few years later was the only thing that came close to that first drunk in terms of feeling the chemicals hit and thinking, Thank you, God, for this miracle!

I was (still am) always looking for a magic pill, an immediate fix to remove me as quickly, as effortlessly as possible from reality, and drink and drugs were the springboard to escape for me. It was my very own general anaesthetic and one that was readily available if you knew where to look.

The downside, of course, was that my poor mind, already split a thousand ways and confused and corrupted, was now put under even more pressure by psychotropic drugs and vast quantities of alcohol consumed at every available opportunity. The substance abuse seemed to ratchet up my paranoia and boost my thinking into overdrive. But despite all this, I truly believe that those chemicals kept me alive. I've no doubt that without drugs I would have killed myself.

My doctors today (an army of psychotherapists, psychiatrists, cognitive behavioural therapists and counsellors) tell me that I am an exceptionally bright man. I don't think it is possible to manipulate and control things so much from such a young age without developing a degree of intelligence, academic or otherwise. However, I knew well enough that the last thing I wanted was any kind of attention at school so I made sure I performed only adequately. I kept my head down and tried to keep myself to myself. I passed my exams and was never in trouble academically.

Most classes were dull beyond words, given by teachers bored to tears by delivering the same classes year after year to the same breed of over-privileged shits. But one subject was different. I adored English and was introduced to wonderful authors by the only decent teacher (in every sense of the word) I had. I don't think he was even aware of it, but I considered Mr Davies a real friend at school; he was always respectful, honest, passionate and seemed to care about his job. Power and punishment didn't enter into the equation with him and he made his disdain for the other teachers very clear (something that endeared him to me even more). He also smoked like a chimney and would often smell of drink as he strode around the classroom reciting long passages from *King Lear* in his frayed clothes. I loved him for the hope and integrity he offered. He was a real ray of light in an otherwise dark and bleak institution.

The British boarding school system is one of the most barbaric, antiquated and brutal school systems in the world. It is truly a case of survival of the fittest with a clearly defined hierarchy organised according to age, size and athletic ability. I was small, slender, avoided sports like the plague and would die before taking a communal shower. I was also addicted to classical music. Needless to say I found school life very traumatic.

Mealtimes in particular were hugely stressful. The whole school of around 850 pupils would all eat in the enormous dining room, seated in blocks according to the house you were in. I was so terrified of the humiliation of sitting on my own, or being rejected from one of the tables as a retard with no friends, that I would rise early and get to breakfast before anyone else, shovel food down my throat and escape breathless to the sanctuary of my room until lessons. Dinner was the same: rushed, isolated, urgent. The only pitfall was lunch – we all went directly from class and arrived at the same time. Food was placed on the tables rather than having us queue cafeteria-style as for the other meals and there was the inevitable scrum of hands and arms grabbing food.

Usually I would skip the ordeal but the odd occasion when I braved it saw me sitting with younger kids who would stare at me resentfully, and again eating as quickly as possible. I don't think even today I have spent longer than ten minutes over a meal. In a restaurant the food usually disappears as soon as it's put in front of me and I can't wait to get out of there immediately after the last bite.

Food was like anything else – an unfortunate necessity to keep the body alive. No pleasure, no fun, just essential fuel to get inside me so I could carry on hiding and surviving.

At fourteen, despite all my efforts, my body gave up on me. The bottom disc in my back literally imploded under the pressure and I was rushed into hospital for an operation. The surgeons were baffled by the situation; they had never seen someone so young present with such trauma. No one could figure out the reason for it, but then again I remained tight-lipped as always about my past history.

Only one doctor, a chiropractor from France, saw something was wrong emotionally. He was a special guy – incredibly perceptive and very unusual. The first time I saw him was with my mother and he took one look at me and said, 'Something is very wrong. I think you are deeply unhappy. Am I right?' I mumbled something about him being totally mistaken and sneaked a glance at my mother to make sure I had got away with the deception. I never saw that doctor again.

Over the next ten years I was to have two more increasingly major operations on the same disc, finally resulting in titanium rods being used to fuse the bottom two discs together, and again the cause was never found.

It wasn't until many years later that I was able to understand exactly what had caused the spinal trauma. I was sent to see a proctologist/ass surgeon during a later spell at a mental hospital, and during the examination he said to me, 'I notice you have some surgical scarring on your lower back. What was that from?'

I told him that I had had three back operations on my bottom disc and that the last operation seemed to have been successful.

'I think I know what caused the initial injury,' he said. 'You were raped frequently as a child. Without being too graphic, when something so big enters something so small it would push against the base of your spine. Over time it would gradually pressurise and erode the bottom disc and eventually the disc would simply shatter, sometimes years, sometimes months after the initial trauma. If the doctors weren't aware of the abuse then they wouldn't have known to take it into account.'

So my father had fucked me so brutally and so often that he had shattered my spine. I guess size really does matter.

Back at school, apart from nocturnal visits to my room by anyone who wanted a blowjob, and the odd beating, I was left alone. I was seen as too easy a target, I guess. I was silent and unreachable. Occasionally the older boys (or, even more excruciating, the younger ones) would wait for me and catch me on my way back from classes; they'd push, shove, hit, shout and get it out of their system. I didn't blame them – I was beyond caring enough to get angry. I was a truly pathetic specimen who had long given up the desire to stand up for myself and fight back.

Each night after the last drops of cum were wiped away I would choose a CD and play it quietly through my stereo. Eyes closed, I would imagine it were me playing, a full hall hanging on every note as I sprinted my way through the Franck sonata or the Bach suites. Live recordings were the best as I got to hear the applause afterwards and I would drift off into sleep in a faraway world of travel, press interviews, recording contracts and public adulation. For a long time I would listen only to the fastest, most virtuosic music possible, impressed beyond words at the sheer dexterity of fingerwork and articulation.

Then one night I started to listen to one of my favourite pieces, the Rachmaninov cello sonata. The first two movements were as glorious and showy as they come and usually I would skip the slow third movement and head right into the tour de force finale. This night I got lazy and couldn't be bothered to reach up and push the fast forward button. What happened next was one of the great moments in my life. A piece of music so breathtaking, so utterly fragile and pure, that I started to cry. Until that point I hadn't cried since the age of four, but somehow the beauty and simplicity of this work filtered through the layers of hatred and disgust and straight to my soul. I know it all sounds gay as fuck but I realised then that there was a place in me that could still be touched in a way that was honest, loving and childlike. It lit a candle that would flicker for a long time. The voices in my head that were a constant source of condemnation, hostility and reproach were silenced and replaced with something so much deeper than words. If I were religious I would say that I had found God. That a man riddled with depression, insecurity and pain could write something so profound and optimistic was inspiring beyond measure. Every single note seemed to fill me up with a kind of magical energy that I could draw on to sustain me at any time. Listening to music had the effect of being plugged into the mains to recharge.

Music became my solace and companion. It carried me through those years because I knew that whatever horrors I had to endure I could always come home to it. I would submerge myself in it like a hot bath, drowning in its luxury and allowing it to take me out of myself to a place of safety. I can't remember a time that I didn't have music playing in my head. At times it became a pain: the piece, whatever it was, had to be played exactly right in my head, and that meant starting again from the beginning every time I felt it wasn't right until it played perfectly, every nuance and inflection spot on, but I'm profoundly grateful that instead of hearing voices I heard music. I've no doubt that what happened to me could easily have triggered some kind of schizophrenic episode, and maybe it did. But God knows I'd rather have a Bach fugue going round and round in my head than some angry voices telling me to kill people.

My last four years at school were simply more of the same, with the exception that my cello playing had got to the point where I was winning competitions and giving decent recitals. I was very fond of my teacher, Stephen, who managed to cope with my insane enthusiasm for the cello. I lacked discipline but through sheer determination would manage to play works far beyond my technical ability, seemingly surviving on pure willpower. I remember one report of his that said something like: 'If enthusiasm equalled talent then Josh would already rival Casals.'

Stephen was a good influence on me. I started studying with him at fourteen. He was in his mid-twenties and supremely talented, easily the most able music teacher in the school. Because he wasn't really attached to the school (he only came in one day a week to teach a handful of students), I saw him as an ally. He was passionate about music, had a fearsome technical facility and I was in awe of him. He lived not far from the school and occasionally I would sneak over to his house to study, and sit in the garden with him smoking and talking about music. I didn't reveal anything about my past to him, but simply enjoyed finding a like-minded guy who wouldn't look at me like a spastic when I jumped up and down with excitement over a piece of music.

With his support, I was allowed by my housemaster to go into London on my own to concerts, and spent many happy hours roaming around the maze that was the Barbican or Festival Hall, drinking, smoking, losing myself in cello recitals, orchestral masterpieces and chamber music concerts. I was at my absolute happiest sitting alone in the foyer at some concert hall in London, a whisky and packet of Marlboro in front of me, waiting for some hot-shit Russian cellist to perform.

Under Stephen's tutelage I progressed well in my cello studies, although not as well as I might have, had I had the discipline and patience to learn to crawl before I started sprinting.

At eighteen I was offered a scholarship to a music academy that could have been a stepping stone to the career of my dreams. For probably the first time my future wasn't looming, it was beckoning. I envisaged three years of cello playing, drinking, living at long last on my own and immersing myself in the one thing that had meaning to me.

My father however had different ideas. He expressly forbade music college. I later discovered when moving house that, as any conscientious accountant would, he had been keeping several box files on me in his study. Among school reports, medical records and occasional letters from me to him I found typed transcripts of phone conversations he had had both with Stephen and my housemaster. He had forced and manipulated my teacher into convincing me that music college was the wrong path to go down and threatened him with all sorts of repercussions should he not do the 'right thing'. I was too cowardly to tell him to go fuck himself and instead agreed to go to university as per his wishes. Apparently a broader education was necessary if I were to give up on these childish dreams of being a concert cellist and pursue a 'proper' career in law, banking or something else suitably highly regarded. I was told that the only option available to me was university, and once again I lacked the backbone to stand up for myself and my dreams.

I chose Edinburgh as it was as far away from home as possible and insisted on reading music there. This was something my father did allow despite the inevitable protest, and to my delight, after sweating blood and performing a two-hour recital in front of the music faculty, I won a music scholarship there.

1994-5

Edinburgh is cold. When the city was being built, the architects decided that to avoid the stench of the sewerage (underground sewers had not yet been invented) they would design the city so that as much wind swept through it as possible, thus removing the inevitable pong of waste. They did a great job.

I discovered after a couple of weeks that I had absolutely no idea how to survive living on my own, even living as I did in halls of residence. Laundry was too much effort, eating took too much time and energy, dressing warmly was unimportant. What mattered was playing the cello and, increasingly, getting high. I started smoking pot every day, more often than not on my own. It was a small step from that to daily doses of LSD, speed and ecstasy. My dealer was more than happy to suggest these drugs and I was definitely willing to try anything that would stop the noise in my head.

I was lonelier than I had ever been. Everyone had told me that university would be the best time of my life: there would be endless sex, fantastic parties and life-lasting friendships would be formed. I remember the humiliation of trekking round the empty halls looking for people to hang out with and being rejected constantly. One girl who was supremely ugly had stared at me a few times and I found myself knocking on her door at midnight looking for some escape from this degree of loneliness. She looked at me in horror as I made a clumsy move on her and swiftly got rid of me. That look of shock, disgust and repulsion tinged with perhaps a smattering of pity was one I had been getting used to more than I would have liked.

It wasn't that I was physically unattractive – I'm a good-looking guy, but the eyes never lie and anyone looking at me would see the toxicity even if they couldn't put their finger on what it was that wasn't quite right.

I would usually end up in the communal TV room by 10 p.m. The halls I was staying in housed over 100 students and night after night I would be in this huge TV room on my own. It seemed that everyone else really was having sex, going to parties and engaging in deep and meaningful friendships. I simply gave up and slunk back into my drug-hazed pit of self-pity, lethargy and hatred.

The course itself was dire: appallingly dull lectures on polyphony, counterpoint and early music (something I still detest with a passion) delivered by screamingly homosexual professors who stared at me incessantly. I was a paedophile's dream – I still looked about twelve, was stick thin and looking for someone to rescue me. Walking to an exam one day, high as a kite on acid, one of the lecturers caught up with me and told me how much he was looking forward to invigilating this particular exam. I asked him why and he said, 'Because I get to stare at you for a whole three hours,' and leered at me. I failed the exam after walking out an hour into it.

Within two months of starting the course even the cello had taken a back seat to getting high. I drank gin all day in my room, tried to deal speed but ended up snorting it all myself, got increasingly paranoid and sick. Occasionally I would take too much speed and lie on my bed trying just to breathe. I would lose control of my body from below the neck and have to wait an hour or so for my heart rate to slow down and the shaking to stop before I could get out into the open in a T-shirt and jeans and cool down in the freezing night-time air. I would stay up all night and stumble into breakfast for coffee and a bacon sandwich, knowing I wouldn't eat again until the next day.

Running out of drugs had become my greatest fear and I became a hoarder. Even if I had 3 or 4 grams of speed and five tabs of acid, I couldn't relax and go to sleep in case I would wake up, use and run out of drugs. So I would often go in search of a dealer in the middle of the night, and if my usual two or three were unavailable I would trek around the seedier parts of Edinburgh (there are a few) with my public school accent and a wad of cash looking to score. I have no idea why I'm still here today – I was the easiest target a drug dealer could have hoped for, but something was apparently watching over me. The worst trouble I got into involved being chased by a couple of drunken guys when I'd tried to score from the owner of an all-night chippie because he looked like he might have some gear.

I did make a couple of friends during my year there; one was a really beautiful girl who I thought I was very much in love with. Nothing ever happened between us, but I followed her around like a lost kid until she told me over a coffee one day that I used far too many drugs and that she couldn't see me again. The last straw had been the previous night when I was driving her around Edinburgh. I'd dropped two Es, a couple of grams of speed and was just coming up on a particularly strong LSD microdot. We were heading to a bar and the only way to get there was to follow a long one-way system. I decided that this was too much of an effort and thought if I was quick enough I could just nip the wrong way down a one-way street and get to the bar in two minutes instead of five. I almost made it, too. Unfortunately, as I neared the end of the street a police car came hurtling out of the junction towards me with its sirens on and screamed to a stop about four inches from my front bumper. They obviously had a real emergency to deal with because they just screamed at me to turn around, called me a wanker, and sped off.

LSD is a great drug if you can stop thinking and if you quite like yourself. For me, although I used it pretty much every day, I never once had a good trip. I would inevitably end up on my own, hearing church bells in my head, thinking so hard that my head actually hurt.

I was so fucked up that I couldn't manage even the most basic attempts at looking after myself: I would frequently walk around in winter wearing nothing but a T-shirt and jeans, getting lost because I was so stoned and disoriented. I got sick often but would just lie in bed getting high and drinking until I was able to leave my room again.

One of the biggest fears I had during this time was the inevitable phone calls from home. My paranoia was so advanced that I was convinced people could read me and my demons like a book, and as I was pretty much always high, any phone calls from my mother would find me hallucinating, sweating and hearing not just her voice down the phone but a plethora of cartoon characters and weird animal noises. On a number of occasions I found myself grateful that my mother was, as always, caught up so much in her own dramas that she didn't seem to notice anything untoward in our no doubt surreal phone conversations.

I was aware that I was in danger of giving the game away every time I spoke to her however, so decided one day simply to avoid her calls and phone her once a week when I would make sure I was sober. I lasted three days before two university security guards came knocking on my door; my mother, unable to last even seventy-two hours without speaking to me, had finally got my father to send a fax to the university telling them that they were deeply concerned for my safety and asking them to check on me. There was no escape from her clutches.

After a few weeks of existing on a diet of drugs, alcohol and cigarettes, I went to the doctor because I had had some difficulty breathing and he had me blow into one of those tubes that measure your lung function and breathing capacity. After three unsuccessful attempts to register even a minimal reading I sat down, hacking my guts out and trying to avoid the look of astonishment from this doc who told me I breathed like an asthmatic sixty-year-old. It seemed that smoking speed as well as snorting it had resulted in it crystallising on my lungs. That, together with a sixty-a-day cigarette habit and at least a dozen pure grass joints every day did not leave me in the best of physical health. My mental health was not much better either: I was by now hallucinating even when not dropping acid, hearing voices, flinching at the mere sight of a police car, and jumping out of my skin at any sudden noises or knocks on the door. I would spend hours lying on my bed, seeing animals come out of the walls and watching the ceiling getting lower and lower, threatening to crush me.

I must have been the only undergraduate in the UK who didn't have sex for the entire year I was there; I stopped playing the cello completely and just concentrated on killing myself as slowly and chemically as possible.

One night my mother came up from London to see me. She was staying overnight in a fancy hotel and we arranged to meet for dinner. Over our main course she told me that she and my father were divorcing and that she'd been having an affair. She went into a little too much detail for my liking (she'd drunk too much wine) and started crying and moaning about how difficult her life was and how deeply unhappy she had always been. I eventually got to the point where I simply couldn't take it any more. I was sick of being a parent to my mother; ever since I could remember I had endured listening to her bleat on about how unhappy she was, her marital problems, her headaches, migraines, period pains. I had learned to protect her from knowing how alone and scared I was from the age of five, because I knew she could not deal with those realities. I had consistently lied to her and shielded her from the truth even though she was my mum and she should be the one person I can turn to. For the first time since I was a little boy I decided I wanted her to listen to me for once and not think about protecting her.

During a pause in the conversation I took a deep breath, looked her in the eye and said in one long breath, 'Mum, I have to tell you something I have been using a lot of drugs and cannot seem to stop I'm drinking and getting high every day and I need help.' I could not believe that I had spoken those words. Finally one of my secrets was out and I knew my mum would make it better. A cuddle, words of love and support and then a plan of action would be made together.

I waited for her response, holding my breath, and after a few seconds that seemed to last a lifetime, she looked at me and said, 'You do understand why Dad and I are splitting up, don't you, Josh? Do you think it will all work out okay?'

It brought me instantly back down to earth and I felt myself blushing with familiar shame like a guilty child.

Once again she hadn't heard a word I said, so caught up was she with her own problems. 'Why did I expect things to be different?' I kept asking myself. No doubt I was old enough not to need my mother to rescue me. I was an adult and should be able to function independently of parental help. The fact that I couldn't simply increased the level of despair, self-hatred and loneliness. I knew I was a failure.

Deep down I think I'd always believed that if things ever got really, truly, completely shit I could turn to my mum as a last resort. Doesn't every child? Realising now that even that wasn't going to be an option, I walked away from our dinner feeling like a walking corpse.

Crushingly, I realised that I really was on my own. That there was no one to rescue me. I cared so little for myself that not even I wanted to get better. The idea of running myself into the ground through self-neglect and massive drug use became the only attractive prospect. I had run out of all other options.

I went downhill quickly. I came home for the holidays and even I couldn't manage to hide how bad things were. I was rake thin, coughing up blood, abusive and threatening to everyone, and a total liability. After several phone calls from concerned friends of my mother who had seen me on the odd occasion at home or out in the high street, she arranged for me to go and see a shrink. I went to see him mainly to get her off my back, and also because I wanted money from her. I thought I could see this guy, convince him I was fine, hit my mum for a grand to go on holiday and hide out somewhere in London getting high.

So I trotted off to Harley Street to see some psychiatrist who had been recommended by my mother's GP. This guy was scary. He was enormous – at least 6 feet 7 inches – with no hair, glasses an inch thick and the biggest nose I'd ever seen. He sat me down and asked me a few questions to which I lied as honestly as possible. I told him a little bit about my drug use, a little bit about the hallucinations, and nothing about my past.

He was either extremely perceptive or getting commission for referrals, because after thirty minutes he picked up the phone and in front of me he called a rehab unit. He spoke as if I were invisible, referring to a patient exhibiting psychotic symptoms, taking a dangerous cocktail of drugs, presenting with serious short-term and long-term memory problems and various personality disorders that needed to be diagnosed. It took a few minutes before I realised he was actually talking about me, and by the time he put the phone down there was a bed waiting for me. He told me not to bother going home, but that someone would be along shortly to accompany me to the unit in Chelsea.

I was pretty stunned. I felt like telling him to go fuck himself, but on reflection thought what better way to relax than in some nice celebrity-filled health farm, piss off and embarrass my mother whose friends would no doubt be appalled, have daily massages, great food and gentle walks through nature. So I called my mother and told her what was going on. Predictably, she burst into tears and asked me if it was because of the divorce and was it all her fault, and she knew she'd made a few mistakes, and so on. I reassured her and told her I was fine and would see her soon, all the time wanting to scream at her that yes it was all her fault, I fucking hated her and a few mistakes didn't even begin to describe the hell I had been through. I was having a real teenage moment in my head.

Of course she wasn't to blame for any of this, but I was far from taking any kind of responsibility for my actions. It was much easier to blame her than look at my part in everything.

What I didn't realise until after I had been admitted to the rehab, was that I was to be kept in a locked ward, and rather than the couple of weeks I had expected to spend there, I was to be there for two months. They put me on an anti-psychotic drug (sulpiride) and detoxed me before letting me into the general population of drunks and addicts who were there to clean up. I weighed less than eight stone and couldn't string a sentence together. The hallucinations had got much worse and I was more confused and frightened than I had ever been before. Rehab was not fun (no shit) – it was confrontative, hostile and to my mind pointless. I kept being asked how I was feeling when I knew full well I hadn't trusted myself to allow a feeling to emerge since the age of five. My feelings were hidden and avoided until I simply stopped recognising them and got on with the business of surviving.

Treatment involved intensive group therapy combined with increasingly desperate attempts to get me to open up. A part of me really wished I had the ability to disclose my past and ask for help, but I felt that I just couldn't risk it.

And I was more desperate than I had ever been to have a drink. The other patients were all at least twice my age, and I was seen as a cocky, lazy druggie who didn't want to get well. I remained tight-lipped and angry and waited impatiently for my eight weeks to pass, figuring that the best way to get through it quickly was to shut up and wait it out. I'm sure they had their hearts in the right place, but I was genuinely incapable of opening myself up enough to get any help.

Looking back, I think that the only thing rehab did for me of any real benefit was to introduce me to Alcoholics Anonymous. Attendance at meetings was compulsory, and at the rate I was going, if they hadn't got me to my first AA meeting I would have been dead within a couple of years.

Formed in the early 1930s by two drunks in Ohio, AA is the most successful remedy in the world for alcoholism. The society is indeed a miracle. From my first meeting (of which there are nearly 800 each week in London alone) I was made to feel welcome, supported and safe. The meeting was in the basement of an old church in Marylebone. I had expected old men in raincoats, chain-smoking and shaking as they told each other how best to control their drinking.

When I walked through the door, I was sure I was in the wrong place. Thirty or so well-dressed, happy-looking and friendly men and women were milling about, drinking coffee and chatting.

I sat quietly at the back and waited for the meeting to start. I was escorted by staff from the rehab so there was no way I could do a runner. A couple of well-meaning men came up to me and introduced themselves, welcoming me and telling me I was in the right place, that nothing was expected of me, and that I should try to sit back and relax, and when people spoke listen out for the similarities and not the differences. One woman brought me a cup of hot sweet tea and smiled at me. No one asked me for anything.

When the meeting started I couldn't believe my ears. After a few readings which went right over my head, some guy who was sitting at the front alongside the woman running the meeting started talking about his life both drinking and sober. This guy reminded me of my dad: middle-aged, public school educated, a professional in the City and a father. But there all similarities ended. He talked so honestly and humbly about his past, the mistakes he made, the shame he felt and the damage he had done to his friends and family. There was no trace of self-pity or attention-seeking, and it wasn't all horror stories; he told jokes and made us laugh, but most importantly he told the truth. He talked about how towards the end of his drinking he had left his infant son alone in the house for twenty minutes because he had to go and get a bottle of whisky, and when he got back the kid was in the kitchen trying to drink a bottle of bleach from under the sink. He was crying and racked with grief. He described how it took ten years of continuous sobriety for his wife to trust him again and that he now spends every minute he can with his son talking with him, supporting him, making amends to him through actions.

I just couldn't get my head around the fact that this guy was telling us all this stuff. And even stranger was the fact that no one interrupted him, no one seemed to judge him, and in fact a lot of people were nodding and clearly identifying with him. There seemed to me to be no hidden agenda, no ulterior motive: all this guy wanted to do was show people that, yes, alcoholism can destroy lives but sobriety can rebuild them and AA gives you the tools to do so. I was impressed. And when he and others started talking about their feelings of loneliness, isolation, despair and frustration I started nodding too. Maybe here was a place where I could begin to tell people my secrets.

After I left rehab I went to hundreds of meetings and stayed clean and sober. I didn't know who I really was and I spouted endless shit in almost every meeting I attended and yet I was told to keep coming back, welcomed with open arms, inundated with phone numbers from sober men who urged me to call them for support twenty-four hours a day, and was not once judged or asked to leave. I had never felt so included in anything in all my life. There was no hierarchy, no leaders, no rules and no sermons. It focused on spiritual rather than religious guidance and when people talked it came from a place of experience, not one of advice. There was no charge, no records kept and absolutely no requirement for membership other than a desire to stop drinking.

It seemed that these people wanted nothing from me other than my presence. I started to realise what being part of a family felt like and it really felt good. I went to meetings every day for the first three months like they suggested, and thereafter went consistently to four or five a week.

That first year of sobriety was the most enjoyable I had had ever since I could remember. I smoked endless cigarettes, went to meetings almost every day and talked shit with my AA buddies at cafés afterwards.

AA is one of many programmes based on twelve steps. These are the stages the recovering alcoholic goes through to clear away the wreckage of their past and rebuild a new life based on integrity, honesty and willingness. I tried working them as best I could, with the support of people who had been around the programme much longer than I had, but seemed constitutionally incapable of being honest with myself so I simply didn't get well.

I wish I could say that going to meetings and attempting the steps was all I needed to grow and flourish into the man I was meant to be, but despite all the fellowship, love and compassion, I was still unable to sit with myself and with my feelings and was desperate to change the way I felt. I hated being with others because I felt like such a retard, and yet I couldn't be with myself. I'd wake up and get out of the shitty little studio that I rented in Camden within a few minutes. I'd grab coffee and something sugary, plug in my headphones and set off to wherever I was going that day – usually wandering around London terrified and confused. I'd distract myself with the hustle of civilian life, hang out in an AA meeting hiding behind walls of words, go home having eaten shit and watch TV until I fell asleep. I don't think I ever had more than a couple of minutes of stillness and silence in any given twenty-four hours. Saddest of all for me was the fact that I had entirely abandoned the cello. I had convinced myself that my dreams of a career as a cellist were infantile and way beyond the realms of possibility, especially given my age and the disruption that drugs and drink had caused. I just allowed those dreams that had kept me inspired and alive for so long to crumble and die.

I seemed to be fighting a constant battle with the monsters inside me, and far too quickly the distractions of smoking, eating, talking and running, things that had temporarily filled the hole that drugs and drink had left, stopped working. I was forced to look elsewhere if I was to quieten the voices in my head and avoid the reality of my past – something I had to do; if I stared at and confronted the truth I believed it would kill me.

Prostitutes seemed like a great way to plug the hole. I always knew that I wasn't gay, but 'normal' women with aspirations of intimacy, cuddles and long talks made me want to shove a hot spike through my cock. I tried, but as soon as the sex was over I wanted to die or murder them, and being the intuitive creatures they are, they inevitably disappeared pretty quickly. The shame of sex had never left me, indeed I'd never known any other reality concerning sex. It was dirty, secretive, furtive and plain wrong. Given that, I found a good outlet for my need to escape.

Prostitutes were the most accessible and easy way to avoid myself now that drink and drugs were out of the equation. Forty pounds got me full sex and I would spend hours trooping round phone boxes in central London calling up numbers from the erotic cards stuck to the walls. In case you ever wondered, the pictures on the cards in no way relate to the person you ended up fucking. The majority were pretty repulsive but I didn't care. Anything was better than being with myself and going through what I was meant to go through as a human being recovering from childhood abuse, alcoholism and drug addiction. Feelings were still to be avoided like the plague.

I remember one particular time I ended up in a flat in Kentish Town waiting for a girl to finish with her client. She seemed to be taking for ever and I just sat there waiting. Eventually after a good half-hour of waiting I decided to go, but as I was about to leave the client (a fifty-something drunk with more hair up his nose than on his head) walked out. I went into the bedroom and there, among the unmistakable smell of sex, sat a massively overweight blonde woman in her forties. Now, I thought that even I had standards. She stank, she was fat and there was sweat all over her. I could have made my apologies and left, but I didn't. I couldn't. I fucked her, trying not to stare at the rolls of flab beneath her saggy tits or inhale the stench that emanated from her armpits. I came as quickly as I could (appallingly, not as hard as you'd think it would be) before getting the fuck out of there, vicious and derogatory thoughts coursing through my head, acting as just another drug distracting me from myself.

I ate shit, drank coffee by the barrelful and became enormously promiscuous. If it wasn't hookers it was lonely women in dark clubs or even, God help me, lonely women in AA who, like me, were desperate for some kind of escape from life, even though they had been sober for a few years.

I staved off feelings for as long as I could and realising that London had too many memories for me I decided to move to Madrid to spend a year learning Spanish and studying the cello to try to rekindle my past passion. I was under the mistaken impression that moving country would allow me to leave my self-imposed prison, entirely unaware that wherever I went I would of course be taking myself with me. I was trying to run away from myself in the same way as a dog chases its own tail – doomed from the start to fail but fuck it if it wasn't going to try anyway.

1996-7

I knew not a single person in Madrid. For twelve months I spent my days working in cheap restaurants and going to AA meetings. I played the cello, kept myself to myself and as best I could I avoided the cruel realities of life. The problem was that one after the other all my tricks stopped working. The sex was always terrible: every time I came (by myself or with a girl) I wanted the ground to swallow me up such was the self-disgust I felt. There were no drugs to cram my feelings down with and the whole concept of AA (honesty, open-mindedness and willingness) forced me to open myself up even though I didn't want to, as if by some kind of spiritual osmosis. I soon found myself in a kind of moral no-man's-land – I didn't want to live, I didn't want to die. I couldn't drink and yet couldn't see how I could survive without it. At this stage, suicide would have seemed like a step up in the depression and indifference I felt about life.

I tried working. I got a job at Burger King and within two days was seriously considering either setting fire to the place or putting rat poison in the chip oil, so I quit and went more upmarket, becoming a waiter at a decent restaurant near my flat. This wasn't too bad and I started making quite good money, but ultimately I could feel myself being pulled back into drinking. Everyone there drank like fish, and it was getting harder and harder to think up excuses why I couldn't hang out with the guys after work and have a glass of wine; after all, in Spain wine is barely even considered alcoholic. More worryingly I began to ask myself why I couldn't have just one glass. I had heard enough horror stories in AA about people taking just one drink and eventually ending up dead, and if I was honest, I knew that after a couple of drinks I'd want a spliff, and I couldn't smoke grass without wanting something to bring me up afterwards, and then I'd be right back where I started, using everything I could get my hands on and fucking myself over royally in the process.

Before I went to Madrid I had envisioned living in a shabbily beautiful apartment, playing the cello while some stunning Spanish girl lay naked on our bed listening to me play and maybe making ravishing pencil drawings of me. I would play chess with grizzly old Spanish dudes as they talked about their time in the Civil War, learn about art, seduction, see plays and read Cervantes in the original language. In reality, I spent my year in Madrid without even visiting the Prado, without venturing beyond a square kilometre of my tiny studio, and ultimately without finding any kind of escape or solace at all. I'd wasted another year running, hiding and distracting myself from anything of real value or truth.

I gritted my teeth and went back to London where I chose to study psychology at university. I figured if I was so fucked up at least I could learn how to think my way out of it and maybe help some others in the same boat. Talk about the blind leading the blind.

1997-2000

I forced my way through university, fighting the urge to leave that arose pretty much every week. I couldn't go back to Edinburgh as I had burned too many bridges there and the police were looking for me thanks to one of my dealers surrendering her little black book of customers' names, so I enrolled at one of the many London universities. I found it a struggle to be back in that kind of environment, but there were some things in my favour that made it possible for me to finish the degree. First off, I had my own flat – a one-bed dive in Camden. I slept on a fold-out bed and tried without much success to tidy up once a month. Second, I was based in London where there were hundreds of AA meetings each week. Even though I still had a degree of dishonesty with myself that horrified me, I found immense relief at being able to sit in a safe place and talk about fear, anger, sadness, betrayal and hopelessness. Even more remarkably other recovering alcoholics would come up to me afterwards and identify with me, sharing their experience of university, family, insanity. Somehow I would always tune out when they started talking about recovery and what they had done to make life better for themselves.

Their compassion carried me through university and I found it infinitely less traumatic than Edinburgh. I studied hard, passed my exams and even started to become a little more sociable. In my first term there I met my friend Greg who was to be instrumental in helping me years later and whom I still count as one of my oldest and dearest friends today. Greg had had his share of trauma and although we never really talked about our pasts, we didn't need to. We knew we shared some kind of bond and that we were kindred spirits, and I couldn't imagine my life today without him there as a source of support, companionship and wisdom.

In part I managed to get through because I became a different person. Now the drink and drugs had stopped I wasn't trying to kill myself. I had stopped seeing prostitutes, although truth be told I felt like I had a lot of catching up to do when it came to having sex after my drought in Edinburgh and Madrid and I slept around a lot in London, mainly with other students.

Instead of dwelling on the past I started to focus more on the here and now and it did me the world of good. They talk all the time in AA about a day at a time, and keeping it in the day and now I could see why. If you have one foot in yesterday and one foot in tomorrow then, as a friend of mine in AA so succinctly put it, you're pissing all over today.

I never thought about my childhood or the sexual abuse I had endured any more and hadn't ever told anyone about it. I had forced it so far down inside me that I managed to convince myself it had never even happened. My denial had made sure that to all intents and purposes I had almost no memories of my childhood before the age of ten, and whenever I shared my life story with a friend in AA or at a meeting or even on a rare date, I started at ten when I went to boarding school and would give them the edited highlights without mentioning anything about sex. Everything before then was just a blur. Like awakening from a terrible nightmare and knowing that there was something very dark at the back of my mind but not having the balls to root around and try to identify what it was.

This denial allowed me some degree of freedom to reinvent myself. I was a student; a normal guy just like everyone else there. I wore stupid T-shirts, ate cheap food, read books I didn't understand in public so people would think I was smart, and even grew a fucking goatee. I had a pretty good time and after three years, with much nervous revision and several panic attacks, I ended up with a 2:1 and a BSc in Psychology.

2000-3

The truly sad thing is that I had increasingly come under the control of my family. Maybe I had never left it, but I found myself needing to prove to them that I was something special. In particular with my father; the only way I thought I could impress him and gain his approval was by earning money. In fact money (or his fear of running out of it) was the only subject on which he spoke with anything approaching passion. I went from university into the City to chase riches and I found I was very, very good at selling. I could convince anyone to buy anything and within a few months I was earning over £100,000 a year as a twenty-four-year-old IT salesman selling software directly to large financial institutions, when my colleagues and peers from university were getting by on a fifth of that. I would buy my parents extravagant presents, let my father know how much I earned each month and show off my platinum cards. I even got invited to have an American Express black card (grandly called Centurion), the very pinnacle of desire and ambition in the City as it was by invitation only, had no spending limit and offered perks like a free £70,000 sports car for a month, free upgrades to business-class flights, VIP dinners at Cartier and Tiffany and other mindless shit that appealed to shallow, status-hungry wankers like me. Naturally, I hurriedly got my entire family supplementary cards on my account. It was as if I knew that I had always been nothing to them and I had to prove otherwise. Of course it never worked. The more I tried to impress them the emptier I would feel.

Part of the twelve-step programme of AA suggests that you make amends to those you have hurt in the past. The reasoning behind it is that we will never be free until we clear away the wreckage of our past and deal with our resentments. If we are still resentful then no doubt we will eventually drink again. I arranged a meeting with my father to apologise for the wrongs I had done him. I was in such a state of denial about what he had done to me that I was willing to apologise for everything and once again put myself at his mercy. We met at a café and I stumbled through my apology, telling him a little about AA and where I was on my journey. I said to him that I knew I had behaved badly in the past and hadn't been the son he would have liked me to be. That I was very sorry for any harm I had done him and was willing to do whatever it took to make it up to him. His response was to tell me to 'fuck off' and not be so stupid. There wasn't much I could say to that.

I can really understand why battered women so often stay with their abusers. The truth was that my father had never loved me in an appropriate way, given me time, patience, understanding or respect. Instead he had raped me, used me and tried to turn me into someone in his image: academic, emotionally empty and conservative in the worst sense of the word. And I could not accept this. I desperately wanted him to love me and accept me if not for who I was then even for some invented persona who I thought he would like me to be, and I couldn't see that this would never happen. Where my mother confused worrying about me for love and was incapable of not speaking to me for longer than twenty-four hours, my father simply wanted to speak to me once a week and ask the same five questions (how's your social life, how's the cello, how much are you earning, have you seen any good plays recently, when will you get promoted?). I would answer each question the same way (fine, fine, a lot, no, soon) and our weekly conversation would be over in around thirty-three seconds. Having done his fatherly duty he would hang up and rest secure in the knowledge that he was a superb father, and I would hang up feeling as though I had got through another awkward conversation successfully and hope that he would die soon.

On the outside my life was fantastic. Plenty of money, endless women, my own flat and my physical health had improved dramatically. I was in my early twenties and although inside I was broken, to anyone I knew in meetings and outside AA I had my happy mask on. I guess I figured if I said it often enough it would come true. I was talking in meetings about how fantastic my life was, how fulfilled I was and how it was all the result of working the steps and going to meetings. I felt like an AA poster child even though deep down I believed I was a total fraud. I had been sober nearly four years and was deemed a success. But I had a secret. Something really bad. Something that was more addictive and more soul-destroying than anything else I had experienced. In my confused and deluded state I started believing that I wanted to fuck children.

I lived on my own and had an Internet connection. AOL started to dominate my life. One evening checking my e-mail I got an instant message from someone inviting me to a private chat room. I didn't even know these things existed, having only been online for a few months, and was intrigued. Her screen name was something like 'blonde temptress' and who wouldn't follow her willingly into a hidden room where no one could follow our conversation? We had cyber sex (another first for me and really quite fun after the initial embarrassment of it all; rather like phone sex but with typing not speaking). When it was over I started to look around this online community that seemed to hide away on the periphery of the Internet.

There were long lists of chat rooms with names like 'female sub to use and abuse', 'family roleplay' and 'daddy's bedroom'. My heart started racing and my face got hot. Hands trembling, I clicked to enter and see what was happening. The names of those also in the room were displayed and you could click on them to read their profiles and send them instant messages or invitations to private chat rooms. I thought back to my fantasies of fucking dead victims of a nuclear war as a kid and felt like I had at last found people as damaged and dark as me, full of shameful secrets and unspeakable needs.

Over the following weeks, I would start chatting with girls (or guys pretending to be girls – I didn't care) and they would share their fantasies with me; scenarios that I hadn't ever contemplated before would be spelled out in front of me. Young girls, eight or nine, slim, tiny little things tied to the bed and used until they were dead. It wasn't even enough to fuck them, they had to be tortured, raped, beaten and eventually killed. Then maybe fucked again. There was apparently no fantasy too dark or too horrific. Pissing on them, making them eat shit, forcing two girls to fuck each other, cutting them with kitchen knives, gang-raping them. After the shock that people like this actually existed and they were in effect in my living room with me wore off, I felt like a trapdoor had opened inside me and I was starting to fall down through it. Despite the horror I would find myself getting turned on by it all. It was as if I were reliving the abuse but was in a position to be able to control it because I could steer the fantasy in any direction I pleased. Even if it was only in my head, there was a feeling of liberation, of triumph, that now, for once, I had the power. The more I explored, the darker the fantasies became. I was too paranoid to look at actual images or videos, thank God, but only out of cowardice for the possible legal repercussions. What had started out as curiosity and intrigue had turned into another much darker addiction. These guys were my new drug of choice; a virtual crack pipe.

I know what this sounds like, believe me. Abhorrent, repugnant, unredeemable. I seemed to have become the very thing I hated the most. I was convinced I had turned into a paedophile, that I was beyond redemption, that there really was no hope for me now. I can offer no justification other than what a couple of therapists said to me years later, along the lines that if you think about committing a bank robbery, it doesn't make you a bank robber. I'm only too aware of how trite that sounds. They told me that it is hugely common for victims of abuse to have fantasies of abusing others themselves; when the anger isn't expressed and the past dealt with then it is turned outwards very often into sexually sadistic fantasies like mine. One shrink I saw who had worked with paedophiles in prison told me that he knew evil when he saw it, usually within a few minutes. Those guys were evil, plain and simple. I was 'anything but'. His words, not mine. I still didn't believe him for a minute. It didn't matter that I had never done anything to act out these sick fantasies, or downloaded any of the thousands of videos and photos available; I was as sick and bad as any of those guys in prison.

The effect of this on my mental state was shattering. After what had happened to me as a child, and the effect it had on me, I believed I had turned into the same kind of monster that I had so despised. The scariest thing was that as sure as I was that I would never act on these desires, I couldn't absolutely guarantee it. What if it got uncontrollable? What if the opportunity somehow presented itself? I told myself that I would either kill myself before it took me over, or that the gap between thinking about it and doing it was too big for me to cross. But however I dressed it up, debated with myself, discussed it in my head, I never really knew what I was capable of. And it absolutely petrified me.

I became obsessed with paedophiles and sexual abuse cases in the media. I would search out films and documentaries about it and watch them alone, feeling the storm inside me rise up, filled with anger, hatred and sexual desire. I now had even more reason to split my personality between public and private. I was so paranoid that people could see what a monster I was that I went all out to prove to the world I was a 'normal' guy. I had even more sex with consenting adults, slowly withdrew from what little social life I had, and with the exception of AA meetings which were still keeping me sober by some miracle, I just wanked, worked and slept. I was well and truly trapped in this hidden world and could see no way out. I even called AOL once to cancel my membership thinking if I had no Internet access I would be forced to stop, but like a dealer offering a free hit on the pipe, the woman on the phone simply offered me three months free if I continued with them. Helpless, I accepted and went back to murdering young children online with like-minded people around the world. And these chat rooms were full to bursting. I used this as my main justification:

I definitely wasn't alone in this. Hundreds of thousands of people were online at any given time doing the same thing – I didn't know whether to be appalled or comforted.

Chasing an even bigger high (of course) I progressed on to phone sex services, paying to have the woman at the end of the phone pretend to be a nine-year-old girl as I fucked her and used her until I came. The self-disgust I felt simply couldn't get any worse so I just threw myself into the abyss willingly. Bring it on, I said to God. Fuck you and fuck everyone. I'm on my own and I'm going to do whatever the fuck I want. Even if every breath I take is one more punch into the ground I'm going to carry on as long as I can. And it wasn't even like there was any relief or payoff after I came. I'd feel even more disgusted with myself; more vile and toxic. There is nothing more destructive or corrosive than a secret this big and this evil. Nothing more effective at separating someone from the rest of humanity.

And then one Saturday afternoon I met my wife.

I was trudging around London's East End and found myself in front of a beautiful, old building that housed antique books and paintings. It seemed like something out of another world and sensing an hour or so of escape, I went in. As I approached the small reception desk, I stopped dead in my tracks as I saw her for the first time. She was the sexiest woman I had ever seen: slim, petite, fiery green eyes and long brown hair. Her skin was soft and pale, and her voice was like honey. She was a French woman who had come to London twelve years previously and stayed here ever since. Her name was Jessica, her parents had a thing for American names, and I felt an immediate urge to do whatever it took to get close to her. She looked about twenty-five but as it turned out she was twenty-nine – five years older than me. I found this incredibly attractive. A woman who knew what she wanted, had gone through the game-playing emotional rollercoaster of relationships in her twenties (and one marriage as it turned out) and who now seemed to be ready for the real thing. That's what it looked like to me anyway. And, damn, she was beautiful.

I made some nervous small talk as I bought an entrance ticket and spent an hour or so wandering around oblivious to the art, unable to think of anything but her.

I came back just before closing time having spent three hours summoning up the courage, and offered to walk her to the tube station. To my astonishment she smiled and agreed. Before we parted I managed to get her number. I knew my hours of sales training and practice-pitching would come in handy eventually. It took me three weeks of calling and trying to charm her before she agreed to go out on a date to shut me up. I met her on the steps to the museum on a warm Saturday afternoon in June and we walked for hours, ate at a fancy restaurant and went dancing on the top floor of the Hilton Hotel overlooking the whole of London. Time flew and I had never felt so free.

Everything about her was extraordinary to me. Where I would look at the menu nervously, automatically avoiding expensive items, and feeling undeserving of ordering what

I really wanted, she would simply choose whatever took her fancy no matter what the cost. This blew me away. She seemed so easy and comfortable in herself, where I felt like a tourist in my own skin. And a German one at that. She laughed frequently, her French accent, still discernible after so many years in London, was like honey, and her skin looked so soft and delicate and pure.

I felt attracted to her in a way I had never felt before. I didn't want just to fuck her and move on like all the other women I saw. I actually wanted to get to know her, talk to her, protect her and even open up to her. There was something about her that made me feel safe. My life was a maelstrom of crazy, barely containable negative emotions and yet when I was with her I felt protected, like it was just her and me against the world and the odds of winning were in our favour. That first date ended with me waiting with her on Park Lane for the bus that would take her home. I knew this was something special because I didn't want her to come home with me. I wanted to get to know her first. This was definitely new. We said our goodbyes and kissed deeply and passionately. I went home feeling three stone lighter, and as excited as a five-year-old at Christmas.

The next evening we met up again. I had gone to Tiffany and Co. and bought her a little silver heart necklace. She was so thrilled – I had never seen someone so openly delighted at something I considered so small. She insisted that the restaurant we went to seated us near a mirror so she could stare at her beautiful new necklace. The restaurant was a new one with ideas above its station and its menu was pretty weird – all tripe and partridge and everything came with some kind of *jus*. She just wanted roast chicken and so I sneaked into the kitchen, gave the chef a £50 note and asked him to make us two plates of roast chicken with roast potatoes and gravy and to charge whatever he felt was appropriate. Jess couldn't believe I'd had the audacity to do it, and I felt so great that I could take some of my sales persona (confident, vivacious and outspoken) and insert it into my normally withdrawn and frightened life outside work. We had a wonderful meal and after dinner I invited her back to my flat. I was only going to take the whole waiting thing so far, but twenty-four hours was a damn sight longer than the forty-five minutes I'd usually spend waiting to hit the sack.

We sat on my couch, both of us waiting for the other to give the signal. I felt like a nervous teenager: palms sweating, heart racing, convinced my breath stank, thinking about just excusing myself and bailing out. Finally she reached over to kiss me. I was pathetically grateful for her taking the leap. Within a few minutes we were ripping each other's clothes off and fucking in a way I never knew was possible. There was no anger, no abuse, no wanting to hurt her. I wanted it to last for ever, to feel this safe and gentle for as long as I could. It was the kind of sex where we both silently and intuitively knew what the other wanted and needed, and by the time it was over I was on another planet.

Afterwards, as I waited for the familiar feelings of shame and disgust to envelop me, something extraordinary happened. I actually felt okay. Peaceful, even. I knew then that I wanted her to be beside me for ever. I loved her and couldn't believe how lucky I was that this goddess seemed to like me. I was safe when I was with her; nothing needed to be said or done, I could just be. And, God, she was beautiful.

I continued working in the City, making even more money and becoming a sales director in charge of thirty-odd people. It came with a lot of responsibility: hiring and firing, training, mentoring and, of course, making more money for me and the company. But for some reason all those things came naturally to me; it was as if when I reached the door to the office (invariably before anyone else), I would leave all my own shit outside and put on my master of the universe mask. I loved the freedom it gave me, and the fact that the guys I employed were just as messed up as I was in their own ways, so they naturally looked up to me. I became known as something of a legend for being able to take over a phone call if one of my guys was getting flustered, introduce myself to the director he had been pitching and close the deal within twenty minutes without even breaking sweat. But despite the money and the status, work felt immaterial to me – simply something I did between waking up next to Jess and meeting her for dinner.

Within three months I had asked her to move in with me and she agreed. I would come home every day, literally running from work, bounding up the tube escalators and racing home, and was always astonished that she hadn't left me. I would see her perfume or one of her T-shirts in the bedroom and automatically feel that I had been granted another day's reprieve from the inevitable break-up. Why the fuck is she still with me? I would ask myself. Was my disguise so good that she couldn't see who I really was? Things got even weirder. She would stay up staring at me while I slept and tell me she'd never seen anyone so beautiful. She would write me little love notes for no reason. After we'd been going out for a few weeks I was looking for a book in my study and came across a beautifully bound notebook, hidden among the other volumes there. I didn't recognise it so I opened it and discovered a series of love letters that Jess had been writing me. She would write them when I was away or asleep and then hide the book in my study, knowing that one day I would find it. It was the most romantic thing I had ever experienced. She would do funny things like sniff my armpits and shudder with pleasure at the way I smelled. I would spend huge amounts of money on her: weekends at Claridge's, jewellery from Tiffany and Graff, flowers sent to the museum every day, expensive dinners, but she didn't seem to care about the money. She wasn't interested in what I earned, she simply wanted to be with me. I was well and truly baffled – she didn't want my money and didn't care about status. What could I possibly have to offer her other than the illusion of wealth?

I stayed faithful to her from the beginning. The online porn stopped, the weird phone sex stopped. This girl had done something to me that was new and completely alien. Jess loved me unconditionally. And I felt the same way about her. After three months I gave her a platinum and diamond eternity ring. After eleven months together I proposed and she accepted. I was shocked and delighted. It didn't matter that she was five years older and divorced. She was everything I never knew I wanted and she was mine. I even gave up smoking for her after we'd been together for three months; something I had never in my wildest dreams thought I would do. She was allergic to cigarette smoke and giving up for her was as easy as giving up the porn.

Jessica had quite simply revolutionised my life.

Shortly after my proposal I fell ill. My lower back once again had given out on me. It seems that the dishonesty and denial that had been rife in my life for so long, together with the serial poundings my father and teacher had given me, had broken me again. I spent nearly six months on my back in indescribable pain. Our wedding plans were put on hold and once again I was taken into hospital for a major operation. This time the surgeon told me that he would perform a fusion on my lower disc, grafting bone from my hip and using two large titanium rods to act as a support for the fused spine. As I was being prepared for theatre, the anaesthetist came to see me and prepare me for the op. As she injected the drugs and asked me to count backwards from ten I looked right into her eyes and said, 'I've been waiting for this moment all my life,' with a huge grin on my face. She came to visit me afterwards expressing concern and told me that no one had ever said that to her before. I tried to explain to her that knowing you were about to be put into a virtual coma, safe and protected, must surely be the highlight of anyone's trip to hospital. But she wasn't buying it and instead offered me a pysch consultation, which I rejected as quickly as possible.

The operation was a success but for a month afterwards I was in such pain that any movement would make me vomit.

As I came to from the operation, dragged back to reality unwilling to leave my narcotic haze, I looked around my hospital room to see Jess, my brother and mother. I asked where my father was and there was an uncomfortable silence. It turned out he had gone to the ballet on his own to catch Tchaikovsky's *Sleeping Beauty*.

Speaking now as a father myself, the idea of knowing my son was in hospital undergoing major surgery and choosing to go to the ballet rather than wait by his bedside is monstrous. To me it had a sickening familiarity to it. That was the point when I knew that I had no father any more. It felt like a release. Like I could now let go of my need to seek his approval and please him. He was dead to me.

Hospital was terrible. Jess would leave for the night and I would lie there sobbing, wanting only for her to return and be beside me. I missed her more than I have ever missed anything or anyone. She was my heart and soul and without her the very air I breathed was unhealthy. Friends from AA came and sat by my bed, throwing impromptu meetings that helped me get through those dark days and nights.

Recovery was long and painful but after a few months I felt better. I had to wear a corset for a year to support my spine and playing the cello was impossible for longer than ten minutes at a time. I didn't care though. I was at home with my one true love.

In the autumn of 2001 we got married and honeymooned in the South of France. We watched from our suite as the planes flew into the World Trade Center and like everyone else were rooted to the spot, incomprehension spread wide on our faces. If I'm honest, a part of me had to acknowledge a small degree of schadenfreude that, for the first time ever, America had finally been knocked off its superpower throne of superiority, even if the cost was so high. No one is safe, I knew that. Fuck the Americans for thinking differently.

We got back to London with our future spread out before us, full of unlimited potential. It was a great time and felt like the start of an exciting new chapter.

Jess had always wanted to act. She worked in an interesting but unchallenging job at the museum's sales and marketing office. I encouraged her to take acting classes and it turned out that she was a natural. I'd go and see her perform in small plays put on by her school and she was funny, sassy and original. She resigned from her job and started auditioning for bigger roles.

Seeing how happy Jess was, and how doing something creative and new had really helped her become even more free, I decided to quit my job in the City. I had some money saved, and I figured if she could follow her dreams and act then why couldn't I? I knew that I didn't have what it took to be a concert cellist by now. My lack of discipline as a teenager, missing out on music college, the drugs, back operations and total lack of practice had cost me a decade of study which in cello terms is a lifetime. Cellists surviving and succeeding on the concert circuit are in their teens and early twenties and I was past it at twenty-five. I started exploring other options in the music world much to the delight of Jess, who was thrilled I was trying something new and more meaningful.

I caught a break and ended up working on the music production for a major Hollywood film score with one of the top London orchestras, and as a result of that began fundraising for that orchestra. I thought I could turn my sales skills into something worthwhile that could actually be of some meaning and benefit.

While I was working at the orchestra, Jessica and I started planning for a family. We went to Paris and screwed like rabbits, so excited to be creating a new life. I had performed well and hit my mark, and one Thursday lunchtime she called me with the good news. I was ecstatic. The thought that we were to become a family put me on a high that lasted for days. I was so excited, so happy, so proud of her.

After a month she started to get sick with the pregnancy. Seriously sick – on the floor for eight months and unable to drink water without throwing up sick. She was depressed as fuck and mortified that I could hear her every bodily function in our small flat. But I didn't care. She was my beloved wife, carrying our baby. I knew it was a boy even before the scan confirmed it. I just knew. I was also vaguely aware that my excitement was tinged with something else that was darker. A feeling of horror and dread started to seep its way into me.

2003-5

Danny was born on 6 January 2003. Jess started hyperventilating at the hospital for some reason and underwent an emergency C-section, which meant that she was unconscious when he was delivered. The nurses had ushered me out of the room and had left me in the hallway to spend the most nervous fifteen minutes of my life. All I could see were the doctors and nurses rushing in and out of the operating room and no one explained anything to me. Finally at 10.12 on that Monday morning I heard a furious little cry from Jess's room. A few seconds later the nurse came out and I was handed this tiny, wriggling red creature.

He was utterly perfect. If any father tells you he doesn't believe in God, smack him in the face and call him a liar. I guarantee that there's only one thing any man is thinking as he waits in the hospital for the birth of his child. 'Please, God, I don't care if he's not that good-looking or athletic or smart. Just give him ten fingers and ten toes and make him healthy. Please.'

I slept on the floor of Jess's hospital room those first nights in a daze. She had recovered well from the birth and was looking peaceful and radiant. Everything they tell you about your first child is true. For the first time in my life I understood the meaning of truly unconditional love – the idea that I would not hesitate to walk under a bus for that little eight-pound angel. That nothing was more important than this tiny miracle. It was a tremendous relief to know that I was capable of feeling like that. My life had been turned upside down by Danny's arrival and I couldn't have been happier. Everything about him was divine: his smell, his warmth, his tiny toes and fingers, his little snub nose, his scrawny legs and arms, the rise and fall of his chest as he slept. The way he glugged back milk like he was starving. Jess wasn't producing enough milk so we put him on formula and I would usually stay up in the night to feed him. The feeling of holding his tiny, warm body in my arms and providing him with nourishment, protecting him, caring for him, nurturing him was like walking through heaven being held in the palm of God.

I couldn't get enough of him, but the flip-side of that huge love was a feeling of terror and anxiety that had infected me like a sudden, terminal cancer. I couldn't bear to be separated from him even for a few minutes. The list of worries that engulfed me was awesome and apparently limitless. I was terrified he wasn't getting enough food. That he was sick. That he wasn't sleeping enough. He wasn't hot enough, cool enough, safe enough. It surprised everyone, most of all me. I would leave for work some mornings and would sob in the car because I couldn't be there with my little angel. The truth was that I just knew that something absolutely terrible was going to happen to him. If not now then in a few months or few years. Childhood was a bleak, terrifying and ultimately soul-destroying affair to be endured. That was my truth and I never questioned for a minute that this was not going to happen to Danny. I knew there was no risk of me doing to him what my father had done to me, but it didn't matter. Something horrific always happens to children and every day threatened Danny's survival. I could not accept my powerlessness over him.

I made myself sick with it. I was irritable and angry. Jess and I argued all the time, mainly because I was so inconsistent. I would want to cuddle him and reassure him one minute and the next I would insist on leaving him to cry and teaching him some kind of independence. There was a gigantic struggle going on inside me and I didn't know if I was coming or going. I wanted to run away from him as quickly as possible in terror at his fragility and at the same time I needed to protect him and smother him with love. I didn't know what was going on. I hadn't thought about my abuse for years and never considered there was a link between my childhood and my feelings surrounding his. I was once again in fully blown survival mode, going on instincts and adrenalin and had my head firmly up my own arse.

In the midst of this chaos of three hours' sleep a night, fighting like teenagers, every day a ceaseless toil of laundry, feeding, settling, changing, routine, routine, routine, Jess's acting career suddenly exploded. Her agent called one evening and told her that the producers from a recent audition she had done had called and offered her an obscene amount of money to play the lead part in a big film.

She learned the script and prepared for the role within a few weeks, and then it was a whirlwind procession of filming, interviews and publicity ventures while at the same time being signed up for various other films and TV series. This was all happening at the same time as we were going through this turmoil in our personal lives. Not sure what to do, we threw money at the problems we had, desperate to find a fix: holidays, toys, clothes, therapists, all to no avail.

I felt we were in big trouble. I wasn't earning anything like the money I used to, and with Jess's newfound fame and fortune I was starting to feel very emasculated despite the pride and joy I felt for her. I needed a change of direction. Something that could pull me out of this rut and provide some kind of balance to my life and maybe our marriage.

After a few months with the orchestra, I had the idea of becoming an agent/impresario for classical musicians and got in touch with Pietro Agnelli, who lived in Venice and managed the world's greatest living cellist Vladimir Levshenko, someone I had worshipped for years. My sales abilities came in handy here – Pietro wasn't someone you just called up and went to see. He received over a thousand CDs every week from hopeful artists, most of them outstandingly talented. He travelled 300 days out of the year and seemed to be busier than God. I decided I had to get his attention so I sent him a case of Krug from Rome's finest emporium, and a note saying thank you for all of his superb work promoting and looking after Maestro Levshenko. Should he ever need anything in London he only had to ask and I would move heaven and earth to make it happen.

I heard nothing from him until my phone rang about a month later. I had just settled Danny down for his afternoon nap. Jess was out meeting her agent for a long lunch, and I was enjoying a rare thirty minutes of peace and quiet.

'Ciao, Josh! It's Pietro. How are you?' came a deep, heavily accented voice.

'Pietro! How lovely to hear from you. I'm wonderful, thank you. How are things with you?'

'Very fine, Josh, very fine. I must say I got the shock of my life when your gift arrived; you know this shop in Rome is for only the most expensive and exclusive things? And Krug, of course, when I get the chance to drink it, is the very finest champagne in the world.'

'I'm glad you like it. My pleasure after everything you have done for us fans!' I said. I was to find out later that Pietro had a taste, as do most Italians in my experience, for the absolute best in life whether it is food, drink, clothes or women. So I'd done a pretty decent job of getting his attention.

He had called me to ask for a favour. He didn't think I'd be able to help him but had nowhere else to turn: Vladimir was playing a big concert in London and they needed access to a decent Steinway piano for his accompanist, a very famous pianist. They needed the piano available to practise on until late in the evening the night before the concert and he couldn't find one available beyond 5 p.m. when all the piano shops closed up.

He gave me his private mobile number and begged me to help him. I was feeling giddy with excitement and terrified that I'd not be able to come through for him.

As soon as Jess got home I grabbed my jacket and my favourite Levshenko CD and dashed off to Steinway Hall. I got there ten minutes before they were closing and ignoring all the stuffy-looking salesmen I walked over to one of the junior sales staff, a pretty young girl tidying up files on her desk in the far corner of the showroom, almost hidden by the hordes of beautiful ebony grand pianos each costing roughly the same as a new Aston Martin.

I introduced myself and to my delight found out she was Italian. Even better, she was from Venice, Pietro's home town. Fate was smiling. She knew of Pietro by reputation and had studied piano for a few years before realising she wasn't good enough to pursue it professionally. I got the feeling that like me she had decided not to take the risk of following her dreams, and settled instead for something steady and reliable.

I gave her the CD which she said she didn't have and left her my number, asking her to call me the next morning after she'd listened to it.

At nine thirty the following morning she did indeed call. She was, of course, overwhelmed by the playing and asked me why I'd given it to her. I told her Vladimir was in town next week and wanted somewhere private to practise with a decent Steinway the evening before his recital.

'Is there any chance at all you could work a little late that night and let him use one of your pianos?' I asked her. She told me to hang on while she spoke with her manager. I paced nervously for about seven minutes until she came back on the line.

'It's done,' she said. 'I will stay until 11 p.m. and let him and his accompanist use one or all of the six concert grands we store and maintain downstairs for recording studios. I can't believe we're going to be able to hear him practise!' She sounded as excited as I was and I couldn't thank her enough.

I called Pietro and as coolly as I could I told him that Steinway Hall was available and would stay open until Vladimir had finished practising, whatever the time was, and that he would have a choice of half a dozen of their finest concert grands to work with.

There was a resounding silence, and after a while he said, 'Josh, how the fuck did you manage that?'

'Well, I couldn't let Vladimir down now, could I?' I replied, weak with relief.

Jess and I went to the concert together as Pietro's guests and had dinner with both him and Vladimir afterwards which was an experience I'll never forget; being in the presence of such overwhelming greatness was a gift from God.

Pietro and I got on well and after a few more phone calls and meetings I went to stay with him in Venice for a week or two to learn the business. We had the idea of opening a London office for his company with me running it. It sounded like the ideal partnership – he was as enthusiastic as me about music, and with my sales skills and his reputation I was sure we'd make a big success of it.

During my trip he asked me if I played the cello, and I gave him my usual spiel about how I had studied a long time ago and loved it but hadn't played in years and wasn't good enough even to consider a career as a cellist as I was clearly far too old and lacked the talent.

Then he asked me to play him something.

He had played the cello himself as a student and had a beautiful old cello in his apartment in the centre of Venice. After some persuasion, I sat down and played him some Bach and some Bartók. When I looked up at him afterwards he was utterly shocked. He told me that in twenty-five years in the business he had never heard someone play that well who wasn't a professional cellist. He said to me, 'I don't think you realise the effect this has had on me!' Then he started calling all his friends and dragging me round to their houses asking me to play for them. He was insanely excited; he'd trick some of his friends by calling them up and having me play in the background while he told them he had Levshenko himself there. Not one of them doubted it.

My reaction was principally one of anger. For years I had tried to convince myself that a career as a cellist wasn't possible and now someone with experience who had absolutely no reason to lie to me had completely ripped my excuses apart. Back in London I played to a couple more respected teachers who both agreed with Pietro. The feeling seemed to be that they couldn't guarantee that I'd have a hugely successful career, but that no doubt with a bit of hard work I could be playing as well as any of today's great cellists.

That was enough for me. Pietro and I put our business plans on hold, and with Jessica's encouragement I gave up the idea of sacrificing my dreams for a safe but deadly 9–5 job and started studying the cello again. Surely if anything could make things better, a career as a concert cellist, something I'd dreamed of for so long, would do the job. Pietro introduced me to a wonderful teacher near him in Venice where I would go every month to study intensively for three or four days at a time.

His name was Massimo and he was a typical Italian pedagogue: he would often resort to hitting me, throwing things at me (cellphones, metronomes, pens, whatever was at hand) and yet he was simply the greatest teacher I had ever had. Within a few months I was playing better than ever before – my sound was deep and full, my fingers had started to work in new and more agile ways and my love for the cello had only intensified. As well as technique, Massimo introduced me to music I would never have listened to before: wonderful symphonies, operas and music by composers I had always ignored because I'd been so narrow-minded and listened only to the great Romantic cello repertoire.

Pietro took me under his wing and was a perfect mentor. I would stay at his vast palazzo near San Marco Square with views over the whole of Venice and practise in front of floor-to-ceiling windows gazing at canals, church spires and the beauty of Italy.

I had started playing pieces that I had never dreamed possible: Rachmaninov's and Debussy's great sonatas, the Dvořák concerto, Beethoven's incredible A major sonata and lots of Bach. I had hated Bach as a kid – it went totally over my head. The symmetry and perfection of his music was, I guess, just too adult for me. But thank God, because now at twenty-nine I came to him fresh and it was like introducing a twenty-nine-year-old man to green grass, blue skies and turquoise oceans for the very first time. I was awestruck. I couldn't get enough of it and sure enough as I studied and played these incredible works Massimo and I quickly realised there was something special there.

I know classical music has a bad reputation. And, God knows, there are enough record labels and musicians trying to convince you to listen to their work. However, I feel duty bound to give you a list of my top five recordings of all time so you can at least have the chance of discovering these pieces if you are new to classical music. So here we go (in no particular order):

- 1. Bruckner: Symphony no. 7, Herbert von Karajan/Berlin Philharmonic (the greatest symphony ever written, the greatest conductor of the twentieth century, and the greatest orchestra in the world; available on DG – make sure you get the later recording)

- 2. Rachmaninov and Chopin: cello sonatas, Daniil Shafran cello/Anton Ginsburg piano (my absolute favourite recording of these works – unmatched before or since, on Melodiya)

- 3. Beethoven: Cello Sonatas, Rostropovich cello/Richter piano (also on EMI DVD – stunning performances of these monumental works)

- 4. Bach: Goldberg Variations, Glenn Gould piano (Sony, the 1982 recording – very important this – his 1955 is great but the intensity of the latter one must not be missed)

- 5. Mozart: Symphonies 38 and 41, René Jacobs/Freiburg Baroque Orchestra (buy this mainly for no. 41, his Jupiter symphony and the pinnacle of Mozart's compositional powers. Very unusual, passionate playing – Mozart writes a jaw-dropping five-part fugue at the end of the finale that he builds and maintains until you forget to breathe and your heart races and the orchestra kicks some real ass. On Harmonia Mundi)

- 6. (Can't help myself adding one more) Ravel: Gaspard de la Nuit; Prokofiev: 6th sonata, Ivo Pogorelich piano (the greatest piano recording ever made, again on DG)

I guarantee these will change your life for the better. Or at least they'll create some emotions that are impossible to access at such a deep level by any other means except perhaps by using opiates. Doing both at once would be ideal.

So there I was, playing like a god (in my opinion) and yet fighting an unwinnable battle against my past, my mind, my most petrifying demons. How often did I say to myself, If only we had never decided to have a child? If only I weren't married, had never met Jess, none of this would be happening. The shame of those feelings only added to the pain. Danny was a delight; adorable, funny and perfect in every way, and the thought of not having him in my life was just incomprehensible. I loved him more than anything in the world, but I was so scared that I could barely breathe when I thought of him.

Things just got worse as time dragged on. I started to be aware of feelings that I hadn't dared look at before. Inevitably, I started using phone sex again and spending money on things I didn't need, doing everything I could to avoid these feelings. It was an exact repeat of my childhood nightmares of being chased through the forest by a huge, faceless monster (my father?) and being rooted to the spot desperately trying to force my legs to move to no avail. Only this time the monster was my past and the forest was porn, spending money, running, running, running.

2006-present

When Danny turned three my world simply collapsed. No doubt there is a link between the age my sexual abuse started and my son reaching that age but I was incapable of making that connection at the time. I was quite literally unable to think of anything other than sexual abuse and Danny's safety. Every time I saw my beautiful, fragile little boy I saw myself as a child, terrified and alone and bruised. I would go early to pick him up from nursery school and look at him playing with his friends. Instead of the happy, energetic little dude anyone else would see, I saw only a damaged, socially awkward and unbearably vulnerable child. I desperately needed him to be perfect and safe and I needed to be the perfect father – how else could he be protected?

During this whole time I didn't once tell Jess what was going on. I knew that if she found out about my past she would run a mile, feeling repulsed at the damaged goods she'd been conned into marrying. I wish I could have shared these fears with her, but I had changed and so had she. The freedom I had felt in our early days together had long since passed and had been replaced with something different: complacency, maybe. Perhaps I had taken her for granted too much. I felt like she and I had both started moving apart in different directions and the longer I left it without saying anything, the harder it was to gain back the closeness we had once had.

It seemed that everything we had together had been based on a lie because I hadn't told her what had happened to me at the beginning. I was paying a big price now for not having the courage or faith to trust her at the start. Underneath my unwillingness to tell her the truth was an ocean of shame. It wouldn't be sharing something with her, it would feel like confessing something awful to her, and I wouldn't do that.

I finally bit the bullet and made an appointment to see a counsellor at a charity called Survivors UK. They deal exclusively with male victims of sexual abuse. I tubed it up to London Bridge and walked the half a mile to their small offices where I nervously introduced myself to Wendy. She was pretty, American and extremely easy to be with. I gave her a brief rundown of things, omitting the most shameful parts. She asked me what my wife thought about everything. I could only look at her in horror and ask, 'Why the hell would I tell my wife? Are you crazy? You're the first person I've ever told about this.'

She smiled and said to me, 'If you decide to meet with the therapist I'm going to refer you to, things are going to get much worse before they get better. Working on this stuff is a long, hard process and you are going to need all the support you can get. Please tell your wife.'

We agreed that she'd e-mail me the referral and I'd set up the appointment. I told her I'd consider telling my wife.

I still remember that it was a really hot July Thursday. I called Jess as I was walking back to the tube and asked if she wanted to have dinner that night at Daphne's, a favourite Italian restaurant of ours in Chelsea. We agreed to meet there at eight and I spent the next few hours in a state of abject terror at the possibility of talking to her about this secret.

As I arrived I could see her sitting at a window table looking stunning. I had a brief moment of wonder at how this elegant, beautiful woman could have chosen to be with me. We sat and talked shit for an hour, and all the while I was building up the courage to speak with her. As the bill arrived I couldn't hold off any longer. She caught sight of me and something passed between us. She saw me hunched over, my eyes startled and petrified, and she gasped.

'Josh, what's going on? You look like you're about to cry.'

I said to her, 'There's something I need to tell you' – the words every lover dreads hearing. 'It's not about us, I promise, don't worry,' I said, forcing a smile. 'Today when I told you I was at an AA meeting I lied. I'd actually made an appointment with a therapist at a charity called

Survivors; they deal with male victims of sexual abuse.' I couldn't even meet her eyes, and just blundered on knowing that if I didn't do it now I never would. 'When I was a kid, a young kid, I was sexually abused for a number of years by a teacher at school.' No way was I going to tell her about my dad. Don't ask me why, I just couldn't admit such a vast breach of trust or even say the words out loud.

She melted as I was speaking and her eyes welled up with tears. She grabbed my hands and pulled me in close to her, stroking my hair and whispering to me that she loved me so much, that everything would be okay, that we were a team, we were together and could definitely get through this. She was nothing but compassionate, kind, loving, understanding. This was not the reaction I had expected at all.

The drive home was pretty silent. I was crying, she was crying. We held hands. Our life together had been for ever altered and I had been the one to throw the hand grenade into our relationship. It would be a few weeks yet until I was able to see the extraordinary damage I had done to this exquisite woman.

I wish I could say that things got easier having shared this. But if anything they got worse. My level of shame had increased to the point that I couldn't even look at Jess naked let alone have her see me without clothes. Sex was out of the question. I could feel myself withdrawing further and further into Josh world, seemingly powerless to stop it. I wanted so much for things to be better, more open, less threatening but I just couldn't envisage how that could ever be.

The therapist I had been referred to was a small, quiet and very loving Irish man called Mick. Our sessions were in a small building in Hackney. They were uncomfortable and unhelpful. I was so dissociated and detached from any kind of reality by this stage that nothing could have got through to me. I'd leave our sessions feeling even more frustrated than I had been before I went in, because I found it so impossible to open up.

A very welcome distraction came when around this time my cello teacher suggested I give my first full-length recital. This was a big deal – ninety minutes of music performed from memory in a decent-sized hall in London in front of a paying public. I made it an event in aid of a children's charity, and got to work on the pieces we'd decided on: a Bach solo cello suite, a mid-period Beethoven sonata (the A major) and Rachmaninov's mighty sonata in the second half. It was a dream programme for me and one that only a year ago I couldn't have imagined playing in my wildest dreams.

I worked hard and as the day approached I felt a real thrill at what I was going to do. Of course I panicked that no one would come, that I'd have memory lapses, stage fright, a heart attack on stage and all the usual bullshit my mind happily comes up with all by itself. But on the day, after a rehearsal and meeting with the recording engineers (I really wanted a live recording of this), I was feeling more relaxed. Massimo had flown over from Venice, and lots of

my friends assured me they would be there. An hour before
the concert was due to start, the hall manager suggested
we remove some of the chairs as in his experience the hall
was rarely if ever more than half full and he didn't want it
to look too empty. I agreed and asked him to take care of it
while I went backstage to try to relax.

At seven thirty the lights dimmed and I walked out on to
the stage to be greeted by a sea of faces and applause.
They had had to get more chairs, not fewer, and there
were even people standing at the back. I sat down, said a
little prayer, and got going.

After what seemed like ten minutes, the whole thing was
over. I had played well – a real professional performance
and one that I could have been really proud of. The
atmosphere had been electric, I had given two encores and
received a standing ovation. I couldn't believe how exciting
it was; I had realised a childhood dream and done it well.
Better than well. I was flying.

And of course the next day I crashed back down to earth.
There were too many fluffed notes, I had rushed certain
passages, the intonation wasn't good enough, the sound
was too harsh in places. Criticism after criticism poured
through my mind. It didn't matter that without exception
the feedback from peers, teachers and the public had been
unanimous in its praise. For me it was far from perfect and
I felt like I had a mountain to climb before I could even
dream of playing in public again. I seemed incapable of
not mentally clubbing myself to death over the smallest
detail; I had become a very accomplished victim, and felt
right at home wallowing in my own private inferno.

The big event over, I now had more time to return to the problems I was having in my relationships with Jess and Danny. In my mind, not only was my career now over before it had even really begun, but I was a hopeless husband and father, a toxic, even dangerous influence on everyone who came into contact with me, and deserved to be totally alone and ignored.

Cruising for suicide websites to give me some hope of a way out, I found a site with a chat room and forums that dealt specifically with child abuse and decided to start posting there anonymously. It was one way of letting go of some of the shame and to my surprise the response I got was overwhelmingly positive.

Then I made the mistake of looking at the 'self-harm' forum on the site. It seemed that a lot of people (mainly women) got some relief from the darkness by cutting themselves with scissors, knives, blades. I remember reading about something similar years before to do with distressed teenage girls, and more recently a news story about a prisoner in the UK who took the prison service to court arguing that he should be allowed the right to have access to razor blades to cut himself under supervision. He won the case.

The next day I shuffled off to the chemist and found what I was looking for: a five-pack of Wilkinson Sword razor blades. I also got some bandages and plasters. I walked back home to a blessedly empty house and locked myself in the bathroom. My hands were shaking as I ripped the cellophane off the packet of blades. They looked evil – shiny little weapons. I felt like I needed to punish myself.

To say a big 'fuck you' to that little boy inside me who had been used and abused for so long. I picked a spot high up on my left arm just beneath the shoulder and pressed one corner of the blade against it. Shutting my eyes I held my breath and pushed the blade a couple of millimetres into the skin, pulling it down about an inch.

The pain was exquisite. There was an immediate and overwhelming sense of relief. A feeling of calm, serenity and peace enveloped me. It was as if hurting that child inside made him curl back under his rock, and my head was blessedly quiet. There was a lot of blood, much more than I thought there would be. I wiped and bandaged it and put on a long-sleeved shirt. Then I made a cup of tea and crashed in front of the TV, exhausted.

Of course the problem was that having done it once and experienced the instant reward, I didn't make it longer than four hours without having to cut again. By this time Jess and Danny were at home. I felt like a junkie as I skulked off to the bathroom and took out my new shiny friends. I tried a little deeper and a bit lower down. This time I watched the whole thing. Seeing the blade slice cleanly through the flesh, the blood appearing about two seconds after the initial cut, the flood of relief. I knew I was in even deeper trouble now. This was more immediate than drugs, legal, cheap, available twenty-four hours a day and had the added benefit of fucking up my inner child. The little shit had caused me nothing but trouble and it was time for some payback.

There was something so immediately rewarding about cutting myself. It worked on so many levels: a punishment for being so dirty, a rush of endorphins which produced a chemical high, the physical pain distracted me from the emotional pain, and the scars served as a great reminder of how damaged I was.

I tried as hard as possible to keep myself withdrawn emotionally from Jess but at the same time pretend that I was doing great and was present and available to her. I felt a duty to protect her from witnessing the pain I was in and felt sure, no matter how much she said she loved me, that if I ever told her truly what was going on with me now and in my past, she would be out of the door in a flash. It took a lot of work. A lot of manipulation, control and energy. I spent every day feeling as if I were hanging in there by my fingernails. It would have been easier to hide the fact that I was using heroin and having an affair than it was hiding the fact that I wanted to die and hated myself more and more every day. I could barely even look at Danny such was my level of depression. Instead, I'd make sure he was busy with play dates, bought him too many toys, hired a super-nanny to do all the things I couldn't with him – play, laugh, explore, get dirty.

Trying to contain all this energy wasn't doing me any favours emotionally. Almost every night as I lay down to go to sleep, my little finger would start shaking. The shake would slowly spread to my hands, then my arms until my entire body was convulsing, thrashing about in the bed, sweating and groaning, legs kicking. It wasn't slow shaking either – no wonder my cello trills were so good; my hands and fingers would vibrate at dozens of beats per second. It scared the shit out of both me and Jess and I tried to convince her that it was simply a reaction to stress and entirely normal given the circumstances. I'm sure that my body was just trying in any way it could to get rid of the excess energy that had built up – human beings are not designed to deny their true feelings.

More often than not Jess would have to wake me up in the night too. I would be so distressed by the nightmares that I would scratch myself until I started to bleed, and sob in my sleep. She would comfort me and stroke me as I lay there covered in sweat and tears, no words to describe to her or myself what I was going through.

One evening we had tickets for a great young Polish pianist at the Barbican. I thought it would do us both some good to get out of the house for once. He was playing Mozart's 21st piano concerto which is horrifically overplayed but a true masterpiece. We got there early and had a coffee. It was a rare moment of calm for both of us and I spent twenty or thirty minutes actually feeling close and intimate with Jess. As we got up to walk to the auditorium she put her arm around me and her hand happened to land directly on a particularly deep cut that I had made that morning. I winced noticeably despite myself and she jumped and asked me what was wrong. 'Nothing, angel,' I said. 'Come on, let's go sit down.'

She wasn't buying it. I will never know how she knew to ask her next question. I can only imagine she had read some books about abuse, or that she had looked through my Internet history on the computer, but I couldn't believe my ears when she asked me, 'Did you cut yourself?'

I was caught on the spot. I tried to shrug it off. 'It's nothing, babe. Just a scratch. Come on, we'll be late.'

I can't forget the look she gave me. A mixture of pure rage and utter disbelief. 'No!' she shouted, causing too many heads to turn. 'That is just a no. Out of the question. That's a line I will *not* allow you to cross.'

We missed the concert.

After we got home she forced me to call both my AA sponsor and Mick, my therapist. A sponsor is someone who has been sober in AA longer than you and has something that you want, spiritually speaking; in my case, Nick had a family, a great career as an actor and a serenity and peace of mind I had rarely seen. I tried to explain to Jess that it was normal behaviour considering the circumstances and more importantly that it worked, so there was really no need to call anyone. I think that was the night she really started to see how disturbed and insane I had become. My sponsor and therapist both said what you would have expected them to about not doing it a day at a time, finding alternatives (elastic bands and ice cubes? Fuck off), and calling someone before doing it again. I did my good schoolboy impression and made my promises. And then went down to the bathroom to take away the pain.

Right around this time I started actively thinking about suicide. I can't tell you how rational and understandable this decision seemed to me. There really seemed to be no other choice. I felt so ashamed that I had even considered a career as a cellist when, to my ears, I was playing so poorly, I felt like my relationship with Jess was beyond repair, I saw no way of making any money or of being able to provide financial support for my family, and I could see no way in which I could ever provide any kind of emotional stability for either Jess or little Danny. I was a failure as a husband, as a father and as a man. Whereas the rest of the male population got on with life, showed up for their families and friends, and made the most of what they had going for them, I simply crumbled under the pressure and was reduced to a pitiful shell of a human being.

The one problem I had with killing myself was Danny. Could I really abandon him in that way? I spoke to shrinks, read up on the effects and researched it thoroughly. Turns out that Danny's risk of committing suicide would increase by 2,000 per cent were I to take my life. His chances of addiction and self-destructive behaviour increased exponentially, and the possibility of stable and functional relationships was pretty much out of the question. It took a little while, but eventually I was just worn down enough to think, Fuck it. We all go through shit and I figured maybe he'd be stronger for it. A buddy of mine's father killed himself and he had turned out alright.

I tried speaking to the Samaritans in a last-ditch effort to find a reason to stay alive, but nothing they could say could infiltrate my self-destructive psyche. My mind was made up.

I made a big mistake though. I called an old friend in New York who I had got sober with back in 1995. Harry and I had gone through a lot of shit together back in the day and I told him how bad things had got. I guess in a way I was calling to say goodbye to him. I didn't actually say I was going to do it, but I let him know in a jokey kind of way that if I ever did, I'd decided that jumping was the best way out – something about that split second of total freedom as you hurtle to the ground. Of course I had sworn him to secrecy, letting him know that I was calling him precisely because I knew he would respect that and not take it too seriously or tell anyone. As far as I knew he didn't even have Jess's number.

Looking back, I think it was a cry for help: I didn't want to take such a final and everlasting decision but felt backed into a corner. I guess I was hoping he would find a way to stop me, but just like the Samaritans everything he said just bounced off me.

I finished the conversation and got out of the car. I walked through the door. Jess was cooking fish and chips from M&S for dinner. Danny was sleeping peacefully downstairs, surrounded by cuddly toys. It was a snapshot of young families all around the country. I told her I was fine, that it smelled delicious, and I was looking forward to dinner and a movie. As we dished up the food her mobile rang. She took the call and then walked downstairs to speak to whoever it was. Of course at some level I knew it was my buddy, ratting me out like a cunt. She came back ten minutes later and looked at me with such love and worry that I just started crying. Her voice was very calm, very reassuring. Harry had called her from New York, and following their conversation she had called my best friend Greg, a very bright psychologist whom I had met at university and who lived not far from us. Turned out he was on his way over. Jess asked me to give her my car keys and sit with her in the garden while we waited for Greg to show up.

He arrived pretty quickly and we all sat in the living room. I felt really uncomfortable and tried as best I could to joke my way through it. But he was trained, perceptive and had two PhDs. After finishing his degree, when I had gone into the City chasing money, he had continued to study with great success and was now at the start of an enormously promising career as a psychologist. After a long conversation he asked me for a favour. He wanted me to call a hospital called the Grove Clinic and speak to someone there that he knew professionally. Jess and he both agreed that it was a good idea, and there was a hint from him that if I didn't approach them, he would take some action to make them come to me.

To appease them I called his psychiatrist friend there the next morning. The Grove is one of those celebrity-filled rehabs that deals with drug and alcohol addiction among the wealthy and also has a separate unit for depressed/ mental patients. I was pretty sure that I fitted into the latter category and having spoken with the psych I could tell he agreed with my conclusion. I spoke with Jess before I went to the appointment. As it turned out, she had asked her parents to come to London from the South of France and Danny adored them. I knew that they would be a huge support to her. I also knew that if I went to see this guy chances were that I wouldn't be coming home for a while; he'd even told me to bring a bag with me. Jess seemed to be relieved beyond measure and begged me to pack a bag and go as soon as possible.

I walked into the Grove Clinic at around 4 p.m. The place was enormous; it reminded me of one of those huge nursing homes where shell-shocked First World War veterans would go to recover after having lost their limbs and minds. A vast, white hospital for the unsound mind.

The psychiatrist kept me waiting for at least two hours while I huddled on a couch in the waiting room, woolly hat pulled down over my eyes, hands trembling. My childhood tics had returned in full force and barely a minute would go by without another strange squeak emanating from my throat. No one seemed to mind; perhaps they had seen it all before or perhaps I scared them, but people left me well alone to my deranged thoughts. To kill time I went into the bathroom and cut deep. I'd come equipped. I'd hidden blades in my deodorant bottle, shoes, toothpaste and inner linings of my coat. Always be prepared.

Finally he called me into his office. The shrink looked about forty; well spoken, calm, assured and very skinny. He apologised for the delay and sat me down. I spent an hour and a half with him, answering all his questions and either ignoring or lying about the ones I didn't like: 'Are you suicidal? Do you have a plan? What is that plan? Do you hear voices? What do they say?' I think he realised pretty quickly that I was cooking on another planet, but all credit to him he seemed to get the info he needed without breaking sweat. He must have been good because he persuaded me to tell him about the abuse (though I didn't tell him who had done it) and some of the thoughts I had been having. I told him about the disgust I felt after ejaculating both on my own or with a partner. I told him about the promiscuity from the age of ten onwards, and that I couldn't look at myself in the mirror without wanting to rip my head open, pull out my brains and flush them down the toilet. I told him a little about school, about my family and about the problems in my marriage. The blood seeping through my shirt seemed to tell him something too, I guess. When he examined my cuts he could see the word 'FUCK' engraved in my forearm and starting to scar nicely. I was particularly proud of that one.

He looked me right in the eye after ninety minutes and said, 'I've got to be honest, Josh. I've been doing this job for nearly twenty years and you have one of the worst cases of Post Traumatic Stress Disorder I've ever seen. You're exhibiting all the symptoms that we see in war veterans coming back from active duty, and rape victims, and your symptoms are at the most extreme end of the scale. I'd like to admit you right away and get you started on some medication to lessen your anxiety.' I felt in no position to argue with him. In fact I knew full well there was nowhere else for me to go.

My health insurance cleared it immediately, which at £1,500 per day was nice of them, and I carried my little bag up to the 'Shh! Don't upset them' ward and was shown to my observation room next to the nurses' station.

I had never even thought about taking medication before. In fact I was vehemently against the idea; being a staunch advocate of the 'Deal with it like a man and get on with it' posse, I considered meds to be an easy way out and tantamount to relapsing. I might be suicidal but I was at least clean. When they put three little pills in front of me and asked me to swallow them I couldn't do it. I called my wife in tears and told her for the first time how scared I was. She encouraged me to follow the doctor's orders and put myself in their hands. My sponsor said the same thing without hesitating. So I did. I swallowed paroxetine and clonazepam and got into bed. The door was open, the lights were on, there were no locks in the tiny bathroom, and I had an enormous black male nurse in the room with me at all times. They told me that I was to be kept under twenty-four-hour observation.

I started to get upset, by which I mean shouting at the nurses, throwing the odd chair around and generally speaking in tongues. And then the clonazepam kicked in. Within a few minutes I felt a large, comforting pair of hands embrace me, wrapping me in a warm blanket and whispering that everything would be okay. I fell on to the bed and slept fully clothed for sixteen hours straight. For the first time in as long as I could remember there were no nightmares.

As I came to in the morning with an excruciating chemical hangover, I looked around and took in my surroundings. A huge Negro was grinning at me. There were nurses rushing around outside my door and the occasional patient wandering around looking dazed. The room was a total shithole: like a cheap motel room with a sink in the corner, a tiny bathroom with a shower and a toilet, a small single bed and a desk and chair. No sharp edges, nothing to string a rope from, and definitely no windows to jump out of. A kindly looking older woman came in smiling like a favourite matron. She looked at me as if I were a naughty but charming twelve-year-old and had me sit down in the chair, shoving a thermometer in my mouth and strapping a blood pressure monitor around my scarred arm.

The day continued in a similar vein: blood tests (including HIV which to my immense disappointment was negative – I really thought this could be a great way out), psych consultations, check-ups from the doctors, stitches on the worst scars, gauze, bandages, more pills, psychology questionnaires, urine tests and, God help me, a rectal exam.

My ass had been one of my most toxic secrets. It itched, bled, ached and was difficult to clean properly after taking a shit. I had lived with it for so long in that state and I had not once had the courage to have it checked up. After the doctor looked at it and prodded it a bit he called the local hospital and made an emergency appointment with their resident proctologist. I was escorted there by Lionel, the friendly and scary-looking nurse-cum-bodyguard.

During the entire day I had said less than a dozen words and got by using grunts and nods. I had no desire to speak with anyone, rather I just wanted to be invisible and be left to my shame. To wallow in the comforting hole of suicidal depression. The clonazepam had completely worn off and I was already jonesing for my next one due later that afternoon.

Gilbert the proctologist was a balding, squat sixty-year-old with ridiculous glasses and wet, gummy lips that were far too big. He wore a paisley bow tie. I lay down on my side, pants down, trying to ignore the inevitable flashbacks, eyes screwed shut, and disappeared as best I could. He shoved something up me, blew in some air, shone a torch, got some fingers up there and shoved something else in. When he told me to get dressed and sit, I did so without saying a word or making eye contact. He looked at me with what I imagined was his most benevolent, patient-friendly smile and told me that I had suffered some internal trauma and the reason I was finding it difficult to clean and uncomfortable was because, as a result of having been penetrated at such a young age, my anus had been stretched to the point where it was difficult to close up after taking a shit, leading to inevitable discharge and soreness. He suggested possible remedies but concluded that surgery might be the only viable option. He also explained that the cause of my back problems was down to my being raped so frequently from such a young age.

I couldn't get out of there quick enough and mumbled something about letting him know about the surgery once I'd had a chance to think about it. My day was getting better and better.

Back at the Grove I ate another clonazepam and waited for it to hit. I sat in the small courtyard smoking and ignoring the other patients. I had started smoking again just after arriving there; I was convinced I would be dead in a few weeks and didn't want to go without getting to know my long-lost buddies again. I believe I had sunk to the very bottom of my own private hell. Here I was, a young man, married with a beautiful son, money in the bank, a God-given creative talent at something I had loved and worshipped since a very young age and I was in a mental hospital, high on anti-anxiety medication with a ripped asshole and a head that begged me to smash it to pieces against the nearest wall at every opportunity. I had no money or credit cards (confiscated), no means of escape and felt well and truly backed into a corner. The bastards had even searched my stuff and found my emergency razor blades.

I struggled through two days of group therapy, which included art therapy (finger painting trees and houses like a retard), a self-harm group (full of anorexic teens with glum expressions and long-sleeved shirts) and anger management. This was my favourite one. The therapist was a total ass and I took enormous pleasure in telling him to go fuck himself every time he asked me a question. I figured he could manage his anger but I didn't see why the fuck I should do the same with mine.

I had arrived on a Wednesday and by Friday I had lost all will to live. I couldn't take a shower without my fucking bodyguard grinning at me, I was permanently stoned on the pills which caused me to lose all short-term memory, and no one had a clue what I needed, least of all me.

My psychiatrist told me directly that he had never treated someone as intelligent as I was. He said that having had to adapt to survive from such a young age had made me incredibly manipulative and there was nothing he or anyone else could do until I was able to 'let him in' and 'help him to help me'. Please. Even if I knew how to do that I'd rather shoot myself than let that cunt get inside my head.

I left his office and went to the payphone. My one saving grace has often been my autistic ability to remember numbers after seeing them only once. I called American Express – their black Centurion card which I had been given a few years previously included a toll-free number, twenty-four-hour concierge service and a willingness to provide whatever I asked for. I cleared security, recited my card number from memory, and told them my card had been stolen and I needed a replacement in three hours' time at their Brompton Road branch together with £2,000 in cash. I also told them I needed a car and driver to pick me up from the Grove, in Oxfordshire, as soon as possible and to charge everything to my card.

I spent forty minutes pacing the lobby and smoking in the car park until I saw a new E-class Mercedes enter with some fat dude who could only have been a chauffeur in the driver's seat. I told Lionel I was going to the loo and locking the door because there was only one exit to it and he could stand right outside. He started to complain but I told him to go get security if he wanted and slammed the door in his face. I hopped out of the tiny window (who said being skinny didn't have its advantages?) and landed around the side of the car park. Walking as nonchalantly as I could, I approached the Merc, slipped in the back and told him to leg it out of there.

Halfway there I told him to change direction and head towards Swiss Cottage. I was having a James Bond moment. Or maybe my paranoia had simply crossed the line. I told him to pull over somewhere around Finchley Road and jumped out and into the nearest tube station, springing over the barriers. I travelled a few stops, got out and grabbed a taxi to Brompton Road. I had the taxi driver wait while I went into the AmEx office, cleared security and got my card and cash. I paid the driver and jumped on to two buses before hopping off and getting another cab to Paddington.

I popped into Boots and bought a pack of razor blades then walked around looking for the seediest hotel I could find. There were plenty to choose from. I settled on one that boasted 'colour TV and own shower' and took a room under my favourite pseudonym, Max Power (lifted unashamedly from one of my favourite episodes of *The*

Simpsons where Homer chooses to adopt the name so he can find success as the CEO of an Internet company Genius). Their room rate was £40 a night. I knew that this would be the perfect place to die.

The room was actually nicer than my one at the Grove. I smiled at the irony and lay down on the bed feeling peaceful, safe in the knowledge that not a single living soul knew where I was. I could breathe for once. After an hour of doing absolutely nothing I got myself ready for the task ahead of me. I took a long hot bath and set all five blades out on a towel on the bed. I suddenly realised that I'd even managed to fuck this up. I couldn't go without leaving a note to Jess.

The £40 I'd given the scary Albanian on reception obviously didn't run to pens and stationery so I got dressed and went downstairs to Paddington station to find a newsagent. Somewhere during that short journey I decided it would be better to call rather than write. It seemed like the manly thing to do rather than just wimp out, leaving a note because I didn't have the balls to call. I picked up a cheap pay-as-you-talk phone and went back to the hotel.

I dialled her number as I sat on the bed staring at the blades that would soon cut through the veins in each of my arms. I didn't even hear the phone ring at her end before her voice came on the line, breathless and distraught.

'Josh? Angel, is that you?'

'Hi, baby.'

'Oh, Josh. Oh, God. Where are you? The hospital called. They think you're going to kill yourself and it's all my fault.

They have the police out looking for you. Where are you?'

This wasn't what I was expecting.

'I'm just somewhere quiet away from all the noise. Please don't worry.' Which was a pretty stupid fucking thing to say, all things considered.

'Let me come and see you, baby. Please. I'll do anything you ask. I just need to see you, please, Josh,' she begged. I guess I started crying around then as her voice immediately changed tone. 'Josh, I promise everything will be okay' she said softly. 'Just tell me where you are.'

'I can't do that. If I tell you, you'll tell the police and I'll get sectioned.'

'I swear I won't tell anyone. I swear. Please, Josh, for me, for Danny. We both love you so much, darling.'

I considered my options. It seemed pretty callous just to hang up after spending six years of my life with this woman.

'I can meet you at Paddington station by the ticket office in twenty minutes,' I said. 'But if I see anyone else there except you on your own you'll never see me again, I promise.'

'Thank you, Josh. I'll be there in twenty minutes on my own. I just want to see you and give you a hug.'

'I'll see you there,' I said and hung up.

I got there within five minutes and went to the upper concourse where I had a clear view of the whole station. Nothing seemed out of the ordinary. The occasional cop wandered around looking overweight and bored. After ten minutes I saw her walk in. Holding her hand was Danny, dressed in his favourite Thomas the Tank Engine coat and hat and gazing in awe at the trains. I couldn't believe she'd brought him. My instinct was to turn and run. Just disappear. But how could I? His little head was looking around and he was smiling and chatting away non-stop to Jess.

I walked down and we caught sight of each other at the same time. I kept scanning the faces around her and behind her, looking for anything scary but saw nothing. We sat down at Starbucks and while Danny crammed as much blueberry muffin in his little mouth as he could we stared at each other, neither one of us knowing what to say.

'You brought Danny,' I started.

'He didn't want me to leave and asked if he could come with me so I said yes,' she said.

I didn't say anything.

'He really wanted to see you. We both did. Thank you for letting us come.'

'I called earlier to say goodbye,' I said, starting to well up. 'I figured it was better than leaving a note.'

'Josh, there are so many people who want to help you. Who love you. Nick, Greg, Danny, me, Ed, Pietro, Massimo, all your friends. I promise it will get better. I promise.'

'You have no idea, angel. I'm sorry but I just don't see a way out. I'm going to ask you to respect my decision and let me go.' Worth a shot.

She started crying then as she stared at me. I saw her eyes

shift just to her left, looking over my right shoulder and my heart thudded. I turned and saw my buddy Greg, the psychiatrist from the Grove and three police officers about four feet from me.

I felt a sudden and profound sense of betrayal. No anger; just outright shock that my own wife could do this to me.

'I'm sorry, Josh. I can't let you die on me. I need you and so does Danny. They can make you better, sweetheart,' she said consolingly. 'We'll be waiting for you when you come out, I promise.'

I looked at Danny and reached down to kiss him. I held him tight and whispered that I loved him, then got up without a word and walked out of the station in between the cops. They had the decency not to handcuff me but they walked me in a kind of scrum, me in the centre, them pressed against me, hands on my arms limiting all movement.

They put me in a car and took me back to the Grove where I was detained under section 5 of the Mental Health Act, drugged and placed in a more secure room. Frankly I just didn't care any more. I simply felt an even greater resolve to get the job done. I was on a mission.

A couple of nights after being back there I was getting ready for bed. The nurse who was filling in paperwork wasn't too smart and I managed to rip the aerial cable out from behind the TV and stuff it into my underwear. I got under the covers and turned to face the wall so my back was to him. I had done some research on the supposedly monitored hospital computers about noose-tying (dozens of handy guides if you Google it) and was pretty confident about perfecting the hangman's noose. It took me about seven minutes to get it right, which was quite impressive considering I was doing it in the dark and under the duvet. Then I waited.

Every night at 2 a.m. they change shifts and the new nurse has a brief conversation with the outgoing one about my mood, behaviour and so on. They usually do it just outside the room with the door ajar so they can see and write the relevant notes in the hallway. I figured I'd have about three minutes which was plenty of time if you knew what you were doing.

I'd noticed that in the bathroom ceiling there was what looked like a trapdoor leading up to an attic space or something similar. It was locked by thick steel bolts going into the ceiling, but there was maybe a centimetre gap between the bolt and the ceiling through which the cable would fit. It was at least nine feet off the ground and looked pretty solid.

Two a.m. rolled by and, running a little late, the new guy pitched up around fifteen minutes after. Sure enough they went outside and started whispering. I shuffled into the bathroom as quietly as possible. I couldn't risk shutting the door because of the noise, but I had light from my alarm clock and could see fine. I pushed the door to until it was almost closed and then I climbed on to the toilet. After a couple of goes I managed to thread the noose through the bars above me. I triple-tied it and tugged. Solid as fuck. I stepped to the edge of the seat and placed my head inside the noose, pulling it down so that it was nice and snug against my jugular.

There is a feeling of immense calm and power in knowing that moving one more inch will be the last thing you ever do.

As I took a deep breath, ready for the final step, the door swung open and in stepped the nurse. Time slowed down. His eyes met mine and I could see him registering what was happening and not quite believing it.

Three things then happened at once. He smacked the emergency alarm by the door, I jumped off the seat and he ran forward to grab me. I was swinging there as he held my trunk. We looked like we were taking part in some big gay rumba dancing competition. My neck was sore and I was choking as he struggled to support my weight. I heard footsteps running towards my room. I gave him a good solid kick straight into his kidneys and he fell. I shunted down another few inches and started to pass out. The last thing I saw was a combination of security guards and nurses barrelling into the room.

I woke up and couldn't move a muscle. I wondered if I was paralysed for a moment until I saw the heavy leather straps across my chest, groin and legs. I let out a raw bellow of pure rage. I felt impotent, humiliated, trapped and furious. How fucking dare they stop me taking my life – it was my choice and they were ruining my last chance of escape from this world. Tears were rolling down my face as I wept at the overwhelming frustration I felt.

I spent five days under twenty-four-hour observation, meals brought to me in my room, with an hour of exercise permitted after lunch each day. And there wasn't a damn thing I could do about it.

Finally I was returned to my own room and spent a week or so making more of an effort to impress them. I talked more, told them what they wanted to hear and hugged my inner child. I even cried in group one morning and did a pretty good impression of someone having a panic attack, having got in touch with his deeply overwhelming feelings. It worked, and after a few more days I was downgraded to four-hour observations. I had lost my bodyguard at last.

A day or so later I sat in the courtyard smoking, hat and gloves on (despite the meds, I still couldn't bear touching anything other people had touched, especially door handles and especially in a hospital), stoned out of my mind on my favourite meds. As I sat there I saw a woman being pushed towards me in a wheelchair. She was about thirty-five, easily over 300 pounds and had scars covering her arms and face. She looked ghastly: hair shorn, at least four chins, and eyes so dead that you could have walked up to her and pissed all over her and she wouldn't even have noticed. The nurse wheeled her over to my bench and lit and gave her a cigarette which she took in chubby, scabbed, shaking fingers.

To my horror, she slowly turned her head towards me.

'I'm Brenda,' she said. She spoke so quietly and so wretchedly it came out all guttural, like a dying man's confession.

I just looked at her, nodded and walked off back to my room. That was about as much social interaction as I could handle. Especially from a fat chick who smelled of death.

We ended up spending more time together over the following days because we shared certain groups. She spoke even less than I did and it was immediately apparent to me that she was as self-destructive as I was.

I couldn't help staring at her. She was a walking, or wheeling, car crash. Too horrific to ignore and so obviously damaged that even in my shut-off world I had to feel something approaching sorrow for her.

After a few days we were outside smoking again and my initial disgust had turned into a kind of grudging admiration for her. I had no idea what her story was, but she looked like I felt, and I guess there was even a certain amount of envy from me – I'd have no problem being left the fuck alone if I looked like her.

We hadn't spoken to each other since she had introduced herself to me the first time we met. Today, however, I was too curious to sit there sullenly and I lit her a cigarette and turned to face her. It was a pretty day. Peaceful and isolated and safe, even.

'So what the fuck happened to you?' I elected for the direct approach.

At first I thought she hadn't heard me. She just sat there and gave absolutely no indication she was still alive. I was about to repeat myself when she started fumbling in her monstrously large cardigan and gave me a photograph. It was of a beautiful girl of about seven or eight. Long, dark hair, slim, innocent, playful and, I guess, happy. She was playing outside, underneath a large tree in a park or garden, with hundreds of brown leaves at her feet.

'Is that your daughter?' I asked.

'No. That was me twenty years ago,' she said.

Despite the meds I was utterly shocked. 'Jesus Christ!' I exclaimed. 'Did you guys move to Chernobyl or something?' I couldn't help it – the words just came out before I had a chance to close the door on them.

She actually laughed. 'I wish we had. A few months after that picture was taken they started doing to me what they did to you when you were a kid,' she said. 'My shrink suggested I get to know you a bit because of that.'

It turned out that Brenda was doing fine until she turned eight. For her birthday present her mother picked her up out of bed and carried her into her parents' room late at night. She lay her down on a towel on the big double bed and told her to lie there quietly and wait for her 'special present' as she was such a big girl now. Her mother disappeared and a few minutes later in came her father with a bunch of other men. She couldn't remember how many – more than five, fewer than ten – and they basically spent most of the night (a Friday so no need to be up for school the next day) nailing her senseless in every which way they could think of. It was the worst possible kind of ritualistic abuse where everyone in the family knew about it, sanctioned it and allowed it to go on for years. She'd had three abortions (of the coat hanger and Hoover variety) by the age of fourteen, and at sixteen she fled and ended up homeless for two years until she got into a charitable programme that offered her some chance of getting her shit back together.

She duly did and got married, having three kids of her own, miraculous given the internal damage she had suffered over the years. The husband was a saint according to her; to me he was just some asshole who wanted to save her because he clearly had his own issues, but the kids were healthy and the marriage was good for a while. At twenty-five the wreckage of her past simply got too much for her and she woke up one morning unable to move. The trauma she had endured was so great that eventually her body simply shut down and she was effectively paralysed. She was confined to a wheelchair and after six months her husband realised that he had perhaps bitten off more than he could chew and she was shipped off like excess baggage to the hospital.

'I guess my shrink wanted me to speak to you because you still have your wife and kid, the use of your legs, maybe even some hope,' she told me. 'If you do manage to come out of this alive then you have a shorter hill to climb than I will have.'

'And why do you give a fuck?' I asked her.

'I don't really,' she replied. 'I just figured that we have similar stories and I'm bored out of my skull here so maybe we could hang out occasionally.'

Made sense to me.

I told her everything about me over the next few days, and the most amazing thing about Brenda was the fact that there was absolutely no judgement whatsoever. She didn't seem to be repulsed by me, didn't try to fix anything or make it better. She listened to me and in the mornings after the horrors of the night she'd just sit there in her chair and I'd tell her my nightmares and we'd chat.

I told her one morning after a particularly bad night how desperate I was to cut – to feel something that was self-imposed, controlled and releasing. As I had deduced from her scarred arms, she was also a cutter and she understood perfectly. After talking about it for a while (they called it euphoric recall; something we were not supposed to do) she asked if I would cut her. I agreed instantly. I mean it wasn't like I could disfigure her any more than she was already. The only problem was where to get the blades from. We were both cut off from the outside world: mail was opened and searched, visitors were searched and trips outside were out of the question.

I love a challenge.

I rummaged around in my dirty laundry bag and retrieved the rest of the cash I had withdrawn from the AmEx office. There was at least £1,700 there that for some reason the staff hadn't seen as a threat to my safety and therefore hadn't confiscated. I took £400 in twenties and headed off into the maze of corridors looking for someone who could help.

I found him on the second floor outside one of the communal kitchens. He was fixing one of the smoke alarms in the corridor and was employed by one of the electrical firms contracted to maintain the hospital's communal parts. They were always hanging around doing odd jobs here and there. This guy was young and had a wedding ring on. He also looked tired and I figured he probably had at least one kid and couldn't be earning more than £16,000 or £17,000 a year. More importantly, he was on his own and so I had deniability should he be more ethically inclined than I thought he was. Which of course he wasn't. I offered him £400 to buy a £2 pack of ten Wilkinson Sword blades from the chemist on the corner and made sure he would do it in his lunch break and bring them back to me by 2 p.m. I assured him that I wasn't going to use them to kill myself or anyone else, but that it was impossible round here to get a close shave. It gave him the excuse he needed (which I don't think he was looking for anyway) to convince himself he wasn't doing anything that bad, and I tootled off whistling back to my room.

At two I went back to meet him and he handed me a five-pack of blades, mumbling something about them being all out of ten-packs. Asshole. Anyway, five was definitely better than none and I walked back to my room with a spring in my step.

Brenda was waiting anxiously in my room watching unemployed TV and we had both checked in at the nurses' station within the last half-hour which gave us a good three hours before we were due to be checked on again.

My hands were shaking as I removed the cellophane wrapper and took out a blade in its little waxed paper. It was just like my old druggie days and it even looked like a wrap of coke. I gave it to her to do me first. I'm chivalrous like that. She sliced an inch on my forearm, horizontally and deep and I sighed and lay down on the bed, head spinning. It was just like coming home; where home is a warm, fuzzy cloud suspended in mid-air, where the problems of the world don't touch you and to all intents and purposes you're dead to the rest of the population. After a couple of minutes I felt guilty about her whining, and I returned the favour. I had never done something so intimate before. There was an electricity that made me higher than any meds could have done. This is what I had sunk to: slicing open the arm of some fat cripple in a wheelchair in a mental hospital in Oxfordshire. Jesus. If my old friends could see what I had become.

The following day Jess brought Danny to see me and have lunch. We told him I was at Daddy school, something I thought as a three-year-old he might be able to grasp. He seemed pretty happy and ran around like a lunatic (which seemed pretty apt to me) while Jess and I tried to share some quiet moments together. She was terrified out of her mind that I was going to leave her one way or the other, and I was trying not to think about how much I wanted to be on my own, and at the same time make some kind of sense out of the utterly perplexing idea that she really seemed to care about me. I couldn't get rid of them fast enough. And of course I went straight to my room after they left and peeled back the sticker on my deodorant stick to retrieve the blade wedged behind it.

I made countless plans to run away again. I figured I could get about £100,000 in total and I would live in some small

French or Italian village in a deserted farmhouse shooting myself up with smack, fucking junkie hookers all day and dying when the money ran out or the smack got me, whichever was first.

I had never been so tempted by anything. But eleven years of AA meetings had left their mark embedded within me. If I was going to die it was going to be clean and sober and with some kind of honour. The irony of thinking about what I had become and equating it with honour didn't escape me. I had to cut extra deep to banish the pain. I was using wet towels as compresses to stem the blood and then dumping them in various places around the hospital. The cleaners loved me.

I spent a total of six months at the Grove during which time I made absolutely no progress whatsoever. There seemed no kind of solution on offer, no vision for a greater future, no hope. Just plenty of meds, TV and cutting. And my thoughts, which nothing could seem to quieten. Unfortunately the medication had royally fucked with my libido otherwise I'd have been jerking off like a teenager all day.

About three months in I decided to tell my family where I was and why. I called my mother first and asked her if she would come and visit me. After asking me at least a dozen questions (largely about whether or not whatever had put me in hospital was her fault or not) she agreed to come the next day.

I met her at the front of the hospital and walked with her through the grounds. I couldn't take her inside for some reason. I knew how low I had sunk but couldn't show anyone else the tatty furniture, smell of disinfectant and walking zombies that had become my home. We found a bench and I sat there smoking, hat on, gloves on, trying hard not to dissociate. I took a deep breath and told her briefly that I had been sexually abused by both Dad and a teacher at school for seven years. That I had had a breakdown and needed to be somewhere safe as a result and this was why I was here at the Grove.

She looked at me and said, 'Well, I'm not surprised, darling, you were the most beautiful child.'

I think that was a bad thing to say. It didn't feel supportive. I made my excuses and left. I felt increasingly angry as I made my way back to my room. So this was my fault? For being beautiful? My mother is many things, but malicious isn't one of them. Neither is stupid. Could she really believe that the way a child looks is any kind of excuse for being sodomised? I could feel my cheeks burning with shame and anger. If my own mother believed that what was done to me was my fault for being beautiful then what hope was there of ever being accepted and loved by her?

I tried with my brother too. I called him and told him where I was and why and he just started laughing and calling me a 'mentalist' and a 'nutter'. Again, it dawned on me that there wouldn't be much support coming from him either. I got the feeling that he was quite pleased about the whole situation; I'd fucked up once more and he was left looking like the good brother to my black sheep.

A few days later I received a letter from my mother's oldest and best friend whom I had known since birth.

Norma was someone I had considered a great friend, in fact it was she who had talked me into staying in rehab nearly twelve years previously. I had not spoken to her in a while and as far as I knew she was unaware of where I was or why, but clearly my mother had been talking to her.

The letter was six pages long and went through my life step by step, dissecting it piece by piece and telling me where I had gone wrong and what a fuck-up I was. Some of my favourite lines include: 'You suffered an average degree of abuse at school as do most people – don't they warn you not to bend over in the shower?', 'Are you on suicide row? What a bummer, but I guess you think if you're fucked up you might as well fuck up Danny as well', 'So what are you doing, Josh? Manipulating everyone and creating a big fuss over nothing.' You get the gist. I have to admit it hurt. I called my mother who I could only assume was the original source of all this and told her briefly about the letter. She told me she had actually read the letter before Norma had sent it. I asked her if she agreed with its contents and she said weakly, 'Well, there are some threads of truth running through it, aren't there, darling?'

I hung up, realising truly for the first time what I was up against. A family this toxic and this dysfunctional could not be overcome.

Christmas was fast approaching and Jess had asked me if we could all go to France to stay with her family. I had told her I was sure I would be ready to do that, but as the time approached I couldn't imagine anything worse than being around kids and family, with no car, in a strange place. I called her and told her straight out that I would rather she went with Danny by herself for a couple of weeks and I would be there waiting for them when they got back. I even convinced my shrink to call her and say the same thing; I told him that clearly being around families with kids in a foreign environment would be very triggering to me and I couldn't face it at this stage of my recovery. The dumb cunt gave me the nod and told me how impressed he was that I was learning to self-care effectively. Truth was that somewhere in my mind I had decided that if I was going to kill myself this would be the perfect opportunity to do it. Stop thinking about it, stop moping about it, stop making half-assed attempts at it, just fucking get on with it and do it right.

I also knew that I had to be very careful because if Jess suspected anything she wouldn't go. I made a big effort to deceive her and the staff into thinking how much better I was doing. Lots of e-mails and letters saying how she was the great love of my life, how I wanted nothing more than to grow old together as a family and create our own safe unit away from the madness. How I was working so hard to gain the tools necessary to do those things and how I really felt it was starting to come together.

After a little while she began to believe me, or at least she wanted to believe me because the alternative was too much to deal with. The shrinks were harder to fool but I was good. They saw someone who was actively suicidal turn around in the space of a few weeks to become helpful, courteous, willing to share, happy but realistic and focused on the long road to recovery. Going home and being around my AA meetings, support network and cello was part of the all-important first step of integrating back into the community.

Jess left on a Sunday morning and I checked myself out of the Grove that afternoon.

I walked through my front door to a clean, quiet apartment. I was home for the first time in six months and it felt good. I shouted nonsense just because I could and danced for a while like an epileptic. Then I walked down the street to Starbucks and got a chocolate brownie, an enormous coffee and a couple of packs of Marlboro from the off-licence.

I sat at home and smoked. I hadn't been eating for a while. I was so disgusted with my body I figured the best thing would be to starve myself, lose some weight and at least look in good shape for my own funeral. But the occasional brownie was okay. I weighed 9 stone and am 5 feet 11 inches so I know I'm not fat but my father had a belly and I would always find myself a few centimetres away from it as he raped my mouth. For some reason nothing was more disgusting to me than a roll of flab. It just brought back too many memories and I wanted it gone. I wanted to disappear. Then maybe the memories would too.

After dropping another clonazepam, I got down to the serious job of figuring out the best way to kill myself. I really didn't want to fuck it up again. I had some pride left and couldn't bear to be left a vegetable on life support with no liver due to screwing up the dosage, so pills were out. I hadn't exactly been successful with rope and I couldn't bear the thought of fucking up my gorgeous BMW by driving into a wall. Truthfully there was only one method I felt comfortable with out of all the options available to me. After writing my goodbye notes, I stumbled out to buy some blades and a bag of ice.

I spent forty minutes with an ice pack pressed against my cock, trying to summon up the courage to cut it. I don't know why. Maybe to leave a final reminder of what they'd done to me. Maybe because I felt that it was the root of all my problems, but I just didn't have the guts.

Disgusted with myself and my cowardice I punched myself hard in the face and just got on with the main job at hand. I managed to cut through the veins in my arms, severing several tendons and was probably an hour or two away from death when my good friend Ed brought in the cavalry. They fixed me up well enough to travel and then I was shipped off to the Refuge. That's why I'm here. Right now I'd rather be anywhere else, and fuck you if you're feeling any kind of sympathy for me. Deep down where it really counts I'm a monster and nothing you do will change that.

I looked around the room. The light outside had faded but no one had moved to turn on the lights. Most people were crying and there were several boxes of Kleenex on the floor. I suddenly felt very, very tired.

Dr Feinburg looked at me with something approaching a smile. It was as if he couldn't wait to get to work on me and watch me start to recover.

'Thank you, Josh,' was all he said before he closed the group and I was taken back to my room.

Although I hated to admit it, sharing my story with a bunch of strangers had resulted in something very strange happening to me. When I awoke the next morning there was a lightness to my being. I walked outside for my first cigarette of the day and noticed the sun, the mountains, the birds. I felt peaceful in a way that was definitely not chemically created. It may sound melodramatic but in a sense I felt as if I had been reborn. The things I was seeing and sensing I was experiencing as if for the first time. The mask of rebellion and anger had slipped away and although I had no idea if and when it would come back it felt good. More than good. It felt absolutely wonderful.

I was moved, finally, into a shared room with a couple of peers and demoted to four-hourly checks. My room-mates were lovely. After boarding school with its own brand of horror I had a terror of sharing a room with anyone, especially other guys. Mitch and Barney were great though. Both younger than me, both serious about what they wanted to achieve here and both open to feelings, sharing and compassion. There was no comparison to boarding school, and once again the realisation dawned on me that nine times out of ten the fear of doing something bears absolutely no relation to the reality of the situation itself. All the pain comes from the fear of change rather than the change itself. We are dragged kicking and screaming into a new situation or reality and when we get there wonder what all the fuss was about.

The shift in my emotional state was powerful enough for me to surrender a little bit more each day and I started in earnest to throw myself into the programme at the Refuge. I was wholly unaware of the extraordinary rewards that were to come to me as a result of this surrender.

One of the things that had been seriously lacking in my life for a long time was structure. And, boy, did this place remedy that. Breakfast was at 6.50 a.m. There was no caffeine or sugar allowed and I would eat giant bowls of fresh, juicy blueberries with toast and cereal. Following breakfast I would have a 'feelings check' with one of the nurses. This was a twice-daily event that both annoyed me and yet at the same time made me feel safe. First off was the anxiety and depression score out of ten. These were both around the seven or eight mark most days. They also asked me to rate my ability to concentrate, my previous night's sleep and my appetite.

Then came a series of questions: 'Has your appetite changed at all in the last twenty-four hours? What percentage of your meals are you eating? Are you isolated, involved or both with your peers? Are you attending all scheduled meetings? Do you have any urges to self-harm? Any thoughts about suicide? Do you have a plan? If you weren't here do you think you would have any urges to act out any of your addictions? What are you feeling right now – choose from the following eight core emotions: fear, anger, pain, passion, joy, love, shame, guilt? What do you have to look forward to in the next twenty-four hours? What do you have to look forward to upon discharge?'

I would then sign the form underneath a statement that was a contract agreeing not to harm myself or others.

I answered the questions honestly because I knew that ultimately I would be the one to suffer if I didn't. In addition to the twice-daily assessments I would be required to do a simple feelings check (identifying which of the eight core emotions I was feeling) an additional three times a day. For someone who had been so detached and cut off from any kind of feeling other than deep pain for so long this was difficult. I guess that's why they made me practise it so much.

After the morning assessment I would have a peer meeting at 7.40 a.m. My first experience of this was startling.

Sixty-odd patients sat in front of a small stage. There were no staff present, and on the stage a few more patients were lined up. One of them started the meeting and called it to order. She then would introduce the person next to her who would provide a 'spiritual reading' for the group. After that we would move on to news, sports and weather. Three more peers would select various items from that morning's newspapers and read them to us. We'd then be read a list of that day's medical appointments with the physician, psychiatrist and psychologist – we would also be reminded by the pagers we were issued upon admission that vibrated insistently three or four times a day.

Then came my first rude initiation into the American system of recovery.

'Are there any new peers in the room?' the chairwoman said, looking around.

A few eyes turned towards me and feeling the pressure, I raised my hand. I was apparently the only new guy that morning.

'Please stand up, tell us your name, where you're from, and remain standing,' she ordered.

So I did. 'I'm Josh, from London,' I announced.

'HI, JOSH!' roared sixty voices.

I tried to sit down and was told once again to stay standing. Then something completely un-British happened. They started singing to me.

> *Welcome to the Refuge,*
> *Take meds and go with the flow.*
> *With vitals and pagers and feelings checks*
> *You'll wonder what the HELL is next*
> *So it's root, root, root for your inner child,*
> *Leave all your hurt and your shame.*
> *For it's one, three, five weeks you're out with no fear*
> *or pain!*

Followed, of course, by rapturous applause.

Fucking hell.

We then decided who would lead the various twelve-step meetings that happened every evening (Alcoholics Anonymous, Narcotics Anonymous, Sex and Love Addicts Anonymous, Co-dependents Anonymous, and Eating Disorders Anonymous). The meeting closed with everyone in a large circle holding hands (urgghh) and whoever wanted to affirming themselves.

'I am worth loving.'

'YES, YOU ARE!' thundered the response.

'I create my own reality.'

'YES, YOU DO!'

'I will keep my walls down and allow others to see who I really am.'

'YES, YOU WILL!'

You get the idea.

After peer meeting it was meds time. Two neat lines arranged by surname formed outside the nurses' station. I was put on Effexor (anti-depressant) and Seroquel (anti-anxiety). They seemed to be doing something for me. I also had to have regular applications of some foul-smelling anti-bacterial gel on my scars twice a day.

Next up came our first lecture of the day at 8.45 a.m. This could be anything from 'Healthy Sexuality', to 'The Addictive Cycle', or 'Understanding Co-dependency'.

They were all well delivered, fully attended and interesting. It felt like being back at school, but a school where the students were friendly, compassionate and helpful and the teachers genuinely cared about the subjects they taught.

Lecture over, we'd move into our primary groups at 10 a.m. These were run by our primary counsellors (Dr Feinburg in my case) and consisted of talking about certain core issues such as self-esteem, boundaries and so on. We would all get the chance to share and having opened up to my group about who I was and what I had gone through, I could start to sense a bond forming between us despite myself.

At 11.15 a.m. we would troop down to the cafeteria for lunch. The food inevitably sucked, but it was fresh, cooked for us and we didn't have to wash up. I'd been living off cereal for weeks and it was a real gift to have three meals a day put in front of me.

The afternoon was a repeat of the morning: another lecture followed by primary group until four when we'd have an hour to go to the gym or relax until dinner at five. Yet another lecture followed at six, a twelve-step meeting at seven thirty and meditation at nine. In bed by ten fifteen after collecting our meds, and dead to the world until six thirty the following morning when the whole process would start over again.

All lectures and groups were mandatory and people were thrown out if they missed them more than twice. This place was strict, no doubt about it. No music, books, cellphones, sugar, caffeine, make-up or anything like that. Clothing had to be conservative, nothing above the knees for the girls, males not allowed to talk to females, smoking only tolerated in one of two tiny outside dens, segregated by sex of course, and a maximum of ten minutes a day on the phone (booked in advance) within earshot of the nurses or counsellor on duty.

Just as toddlers need boundaries around what is and is not acceptable, I sure as hell needed the same thing here. If they had given me an inch I'd have been out of there like a shot. As it was I was actually starting to enjoy it somewhat.

Having spent a full week in the programme proper and having woken up to some extent from my depressive stupor, I was encouraged by the staff to take the next step of the programme. Survivor's Week.

The Refuge figures, and it makes sense to me, that all the trauma in our early life sets up the template for addiction, abusive behaviour and depression that we suffer as adults. So during Survivor's Week the focus is solely on life up to the age of seventeen. We are put into groups of five or six and allocated a therapist to run the week-long experience. The days run from 8.30 a.m. until 6 p.m. with a short break for lunch and during the entire week we are allowed no contact with other peers or the outside world.

The night before we started I was given some homework to do in preparation: a family of origin questionnaire which provided the therapist with an exhaustive history of my family together with birth orders, diseases (mental or otherwise), ages, occupations and so on. I was also asked to fill out a sheet listing all the abuse I had suffered up until the age of seventeen. The abuse was categorised into four groups: emotional, physical, sexual and spiritual. We were given three sheets and I had to go back and ask for two more.

It took me nearly five hours to provide brief details of the abuse I had suffered and seeing it in black and white for the first time had a devastating effect on me. Up until this point I had blamed myself for pretty much everything that had happened to me. I was the bad kid, the manipulator, the flirt, the rebellious shit and it was no wonder I had been abused so much. I had read books about the inner child, and one of the decent therapists at the Grove had tried to get me to connect with that little boy inside me.

Unfortunately I hated that kid with such a passion that I simply wanted him dead. I had no desire to nurture him, recognise him, listen to him or get to know him. I wanted him to die slowly and painfully and then kick him around a bit and shit on his head just for fun.

But looking at the pages in front of me I felt a flood of sadness well up inside. I felt that perhaps I could have justified a page or two of abuse as my fault but five pages of incident after incident of brutal neglect, violence, rape, bullying and abandonment from the people who were supposed to love me was too much to accept. I kept thinking of Danny and how if anyone I knew perpetrated even one of those incidents upon him I wouldn't hesitate to kill them. As a little boy, at least initially, wasn't I just the same as Danny? Innocent, valuable, lovable, perfect?

The next morning after a difficult night's sleep I made my way down to the building housing the survivor's groups. I had been plagued with nightmares for many years but the previous night's were particularly real and disturbing. I knew that something deep down had been stirred up. Like shoving a spade in a bucket of water with sand in the bottom, something had mixed everything up and my psyche was rocking and rolling with memories, feelings, fears and unease.

I'm not going to talk about what happened with the five other members of my group. We took a vow of confidentiality that for once really meant something. What I will say is that I have never met a more courageous, honest and strong bunch of people in my life.

It will never cease to astound me what innovative, perverse and genuinely evil tortures the human race is capable of. Especially horrific when perpetrated by a parent to a child. I believe now that suffering can create a foundation of strength and ultimately peace; I just wish that there was an easier, softer way to that peace. But as Proust wrote: 'We are healed of a suffering only by experiencing it to the full.' I read that in a self-help book, and found it of some comfort.

The therapist leading the group was a Vietnam vet called Ron. He had a ponytail, several tattoos, and a large, imposing, muscular frame. And yet he radiated a sense of peace, joy and love. He had clearly experienced his suffering to the full and emerged a better man for it. He had quite a following there and would come in at five thirty every morning to teach a t'ai chi class. A couple of people had told me how lucky I was to have him leading my group. I was wary as hell.

For some reason, Ron had decided that I was to be the first to go in our group. As I took my chair in the centre of the room he sat quietly looking over the notes I had written. He looked at me kindly and said, 'Your father was a sick, evil motherfucker, Josh. What he did to you was wrong, was nothing to do with you, and came from his utter lack of shame. He passed the shame he should have felt on to you, and you have been carrying it with you ever since.'

I sat there not wanting to hear this. He was talking about my father, and although I had started crying like a total pussy despite my best efforts to control myself, I could not accept what he had said. Even after my father had abandoned me in hospital during my back operation in favour of the ballet and I vowed that he was dead to me, he still evidently had a grip on me that was proving next to impossible to cast off.

'Bullshit. He was my father,' I said.

'And he was evil,' replied Ron. 'He shouldn't have done what he did to you.'

'Not true. He could do whatever he wanted to me. I was his son. I deserved whatever I got.' I couldn't help myself. This was coming from somewhere deep inside and I genuinely believed it.

'Would you do the same things to Danny?' he asked.

'No, of course not.'

'What if someone else did those things to Danny? Forced him to suck them off. Penetrated him. Damaged his insides. Shamed him, blamed him and used him. What would you do then?'

'I'd kill him.'

'Damn right. And so would I. And yet all of those things happened to you and it was okay? You deserved it?'

'That's just what happened.'

Ron looked at me in silence for a long moment. My sobs were the only noise in the room, my head was buried in my hands and I was shaking. I started pulling my hair out in clumps. Anything to stop the pain.

'Josh, do you know what the betrayal bond is?' he asked.

I couldn't answer.

'It is what happens when the abuser is so powerful, has so much authority that the victim would often sooner die than admit that this Godlike figure had done something so terrible. It is easier for your psyche to take the blame yourself and punish you for it than it is to admit what your father did was absolutely and inexcusably wrong. Does that make sense to you?'

I nodded. I knew if it was my fault I could punish myself. I couldn't punish my father.

'Josh, I want you to close your eyes and invite your father into the room. Call out to him and imagine him walking in here in front of you. I promise you that he won't do anything to you – we're all here to protect you.'

I sat for a while, embarrassed and scared then said, 'Dad. Come in here for a minute.'

'Good,' said Ron. 'Now tell me, what does he look like?'

'He's wearing a suit, tie, hands in his pocket. Cocky and obviously better than all of us. He's smirking,' I said.

'Well, tell him to stop doing that and sit down.'

'Stop smirking, Dad. This is important. Take your hands out of your pockets and sit down,' I said. I was starting to warm up. I had never spoken to my father like this before, alive or dead.

'Good. Now I want you to tell him how you feel about what he did to you. That it was wrong,' he instructed.

I was silent. There was still too much resistance.

'I can't. I was his son. He could do whatever he wanted to me. I didn't stop him. He believed he was doing the right thing,' I said, desperately trying to justify and not betray my father.

'I don't think you really believe that, Josh. Look deep inside, get in touch with that little boy and have him speak out to your father.'

I tried to make that connection and focus on my little dude. I could sense him inside me, furious, frustrated and appalled at my betrayal of his truth.

'Dad, what you did to me was not right. It hurt.' Damn, this was difficult. But I pressed on. 'I was scared of you. I dreaded your visits. Every time I was near you or thought of you I shuddered with repulsion, fear and disgust. When you did what you did to me you robbed me of my childhood. You stained my soul. You destroyed any chance of a happy, healthy life for me.' It all came out in one big breath.

'What did he do to you, Josh?'

'He fucked me.'

'Tell him that.'

'You fucked me. You used me. You raped me. You shamed, humiliated, hurt, betrayed, invaded, denigrated and violated me. And it was wrong. All of it. You were much, much bigger than me.' I was starting to get into it now. 'You had a duty to protect, love and nurture me and you abused that right and used me to fulfil your sick, evil fantasies. If you were alive, I wouldn't ever want to see you again. I wouldn't ever want you to have contact with my son or my family. You are nothing to me and I am better off without you.'

Damn, that felt good.

'Josh, now ask him to leave.'

'Get the fuck out of here, Dad, and don't ever come back,' I said.

'Now I'm going to give you something,' said Ron and I felt something being placed into my hands. I opened my eyes and saw a short, heavy, wooden bat. In front of me he had placed a large rubber rectangle, solid and about the size of a small trampoline.

'I want you to say that what he did was wrong, and every time you say it I want you to hit the block,' he told me.

I took a deep breath. Lifting the bat high above my head, I said, 'What he did to me was WRONG!' and slammed it down on to the block.

'Louder.'

'WHAT HE DID TO ME WAS WRONG!' Another slam.

'WRONG!' Slam.

'I HATED IT!' Slam.

'IT HURT!' Slam.

'IT WAS NOT MY FAULT!' Slam.

And then I just went to town, screaming, hitting the block, panting with the exertion. Tears, sweat and snot flew but I didn't care. My inhibitions had evaporated.

After ten minutes I was spent. Exhausted. Ron gave me a towel and said, 'Now I want you to wipe off all that shame that he passed on to you. That wasn't yours and doesn't belong inside you.'

Made sense to me. I scrubbed, rubbed and cleansed myself. Then he led me outside and told me to throw the towel away. I hurled it out over the fence and into the desert and walked back inside.

I felt about two stone lighter.

We repeated the process with Mr Sperring, my gym teacher. I had made a report to the police about him a few weeks previously while still in London and that was when I discovered he had been using an assumed name and was proving impossible to track down. The eighties were something of a lifeline for paedophiles. No records, no checks, no nothing. But I still gave it both barrels and threw him back all his bullshit and blame that had dominated my life for so long.

After the process, Ron looked at me and told me that what I had endured reminded him so much of his experiences in Vietnam. Going from day to day, hour to hour in fully blown survival mode, not sure if he would live or die, no way out, no respite. I was as much a veteran as he was, he said. Only my war had lasted over twenty-five years.

I finished that week with an even stronger sense of being reborn. A big part of me had died in that room. The deep internal belief that somehow I was to blame for everything that had happened to me and that I was an evil, tainted soul had been brought out into the light and had evaporated. It had taken time, perseverance and patience from Ron and the group as a whole but it had happened and I felt liberated. But I also noticed a gnawing discomfort that emerged during the weekend immediately afterwards.

Sure, that black sludge had been scooped out and thrown away but what was left? I was walking around with what felt like a huge hole inside me and hadn't the faintest idea what to fill it up with. I felt the cold tentacles of depression start to creep up the back of my neck and had a strong urge to run away again. In truth I think I had just glimpsed for the first time that I didn't need to be a victim any longer and the thought of having to take responsibility for my own actions absolutely terrified me.

By the time Monday morning rolled around I seemed to have taken several steps backwards. That feeling only intensified when I found out that the following week was 'family week' and I was asked to invite Jess over to participate. I refused immediately when Dr Feinburg made the suggestion that she come. No way would I allow her to see me in this state, leave Danny for a week with the nanny and sit with me for five days letting me know what she thought about me. In fact, since arriving at the Refuge and deciding that maybe I actually wanted to live, I had figured that this could be a great time to walk away from the marriage and set her free.

I could rent a small flat in London with a room for Danny to stay over, could do what I wanted, when I wanted and if that involved self-harm, curling up in a ball depressed and fucking an assortment of damaged and needy women then so much the better.

Jess had e-mailed me suggesting that we didn't have any contact for the first few weeks while I settled down; she told me that she couldn't handle the terror at not knowing from one moment to the next if I would be alive or dead and that in order to function as a mother and finish preparing for her new movies she needed that space between us. I would have agreed with her had I been in the least bit rational at the time but what I heard was, 'Josh, you're a toxic, destructive influence on our family. You're not fit to be a husband let alone a father and stay the fuck out of our lives.' Now that made a lot more sense to me and fitted right in with my distorted reality. It was also another excellent reason not to invite her for family week.

Dr Feinburg asked me if I would be willing to agree to a conference call between Jess, myself and him and ask her to come over. It took a lot of persuasion but I agreed for one reason. He explained to me that if I was such a toxic influence on them and had caused them so much damage then she should be entitled to come and express that to me face to face. He knew just which buttons to push; in effect he had just handed me another club to beat myself over the head with. What could be more attractive to a professional victim like me than having my wife outline the catastrophic damage I had caused her in front of a group of people? So, albeit sullenly, I agreed. I told him I didn't even want to speak with her; he could make the call himself and deal directly with her. If she wanted to come, fine; if not it was an even greater excuse to cut and run.

I went straight from his office to the public phone and called the Ritz Carlton in Phoenix. I booked a suite there for one month, starting the day family week was supposed to start. I then called the fanciest car hire place I could find and booked a Mercedes SL55 for the month too. I figured if Jess didn't come it would be all the proof I needed that she hated me and I could just disappear. I'd fuck my way around Phoenix, drive up to Vegas, and ultimately go out in a blaze of glory once the month was up.

I was back in Josh world, running in automatic survival mode. The transition was seamless and the hope and support I had felt the previous couple of weeks was but a distant memory.

r Feinburg told me that Jess was thinking about it and would let him know soon. I e-mailed her immediately and listed all the reasons why I didn't think she should come. I included a large helping of guilt by explaining how damaging it would be for Danny if both she and I were away from him at the same time. I was praying for the excuse I needed to disappear.

I then e-mailed my dear friend Ed and did my best to manipulate him into wiring some funds into my account to cover my last month alive. I told him I was thinking of checking into a small motel, doing some travelling to see the sights and going to the Refuge as a day patient for regular therapy and needed a few thousand dollars to make it happen. I called on our years of friendship and practically begged him to do it. I figured even if he refused I could just put everything on a card and leave the bill for Jess to deal with when I'd gone. I had given up any pretence at caring.

What I didn't know at the time was that Jess was worried sick about me. She did everything she could to arrange flights, hotels, babysitters, play dates for Danny and she rescheduled all her appointments so that she could be there the following week. She even had a friend lend our nanny a dog so that Danny would have a nice distraction while she was away. He adores dogs and he felt like it was Christmas when he came back home from school to see this adorable black Labrador curled up on his bed wagging its tail. I am still today astonished at the level of insanity I had sunk to, and the power of the cognitive distortions that were rampant in my mind.

When I was told she would be there in a few days I was like a chicken with its head cut off. Panicky, depressed, anxious and terrified all at once. I cancelled the car and the hotel and begged Dr Well for more clonazepam. It had taken me two long and painful weeks to come off it when I first arrived there but despite the shits, sweats, hallucinations and shakes I needed something to relieve the impending horror. He refused and offered to increase my anti-anxiety meds which simply made me feel both tired and lethargic at the same time. Kind of like waking up from a deep sleep and seeing the house is on fire but being too fucked to do anything about it.

At eight fifteen on Monday morning I was waiting in the cafeteria. I had shaved, changed my clothes and even had a haircut. A small chink of hope had opened up in me that thought just maybe we would see each other for the first time in months and both be instantly transported back to the happier times we had shared. We could be together again in our safe little world and the wreckage of this past year would be forgotten in a flash. But this wasn't a Disney film. I saw her appear and felt nothing. She saw me and didn't even break a smile. We had an awkward hug and walked together down to the lecture hall.

I was still reeling from the shock at the total indifference I felt at being with Jess. There was no physical attraction, no emotional bond, just a strong desire to run as fast and as far as I could to get the fuck away from her. The morning lecture was something about being relational, whatever the hell that meant, and it barely registered with me. The fun only really started when we divided up into our groups (with my peers Brian, Mandy, Candice, Scott and Jennifer and their various combinations of children, partners and parents).

We sat around nervously while the family therapist Kim introduced herself and Dr Feinburg said hello to the family members he hadn't yet met. As luck would have it he then asked me to come up to the front of the group and sit in the 'listening chair'. So I was up first. I figured that if it went the way I expected it to go then maybe I could rebook the hotel and car and be there by dinner-time. Believe me, I would rather have been anywhere on this planet than sitting there in the chair waiting for the axe to fall.

Kim invited Jess up to the 'talking chair' and explained how the process worked.

'Now, Josh, this is an opportunity for you to listen with curiosity to Jessica and get to know her reality. She is going to reveal to you her thoughts about certain things and I want you to listen carefully. After she has finished with each statement I want you to consider it and then choose one of the three responses from this board.'

I looked up at the board:

- 1. I have the same perception and about that I feel . . .

- 2. I have a different perception – would you like to hear what it is?

- 3. I am confused and would like more information about . . .

Seemed simple enough to me.

'Now I want you to make sure your boundaries are in place. This is not about you as a person, Josh, it is about your actions and their effect on Jessica. If what she says impacts you in any way I want you to acknowledge what you feel about it and either take it into your boundary if it is true for you, throw it away if it is untrue, or place it on your shoulder for later reflection if you are unsure. I don't want to hear any justifications or explanations. Remember this is a wonderful opportunity for you to get to know your wife. Are you ready?'

I nodded mutely.

'Okay then.' Kim handed two sheets of paper to Jess. I could recognise her handwriting instantly. I guess they'd given her homework to do and she had come prepared with her ammunition.

'Now, Jessica, I want you to find the most painful example on the list that you wrote and read it out word for word. Can you do that?'

She nodded.

'In your own time,' said Kim gently.

Jess paused, trying to get her thoughts together.

She took a deep breath.

'Josh,' she started, 'when you walled off from me and I had to find out from one of your friends that you were planning to kill yourself, I made up my mind that you couldn't bear to live any more and there was nothing I could do to save you, and about that I feel pain and fear.'

'Thank you, Jessica,' Kim said, taking the sheets away from her.

'Now, Josh, using the board, please respond.'

I looked at Jess. Has it really come to this? I wondered. Have we sunk so low?

'I have the same perception and about that I feel shame and guilt.'

'I feel shame because . . . ?' asked Kim.

'Because I am too damaged to be around you and too toxic to be a part of your life,' I said, stating the obvious.

'I feel guilt because . . . ?'

'Because I would rather abandon you and Danny than expose you to that kind of pain.'

'Thank you, Josh. I'm now going to check in with Jessica for a minute. Is that okay?'

'Sure,' I said, looking around at the silent, intent faces of my group.

'Jessica. I'd like you to tell Josh directly what it would be like if he died. What you would miss and how you would feel,' said Kim.

Jess stared into my eyes and I could see the tears pouring down her face.

'Josh, you're everything to us. Danny and I love you so much. If you died I would never recover from it. Danny would grow up without a father and I would lose my best friend.' She was sobbing hard now.

'There is so much I would miss. So much, darling. Hearing you play the cello, eating dinner watching our favourite shows, seeing you chase after Danny in the park, watching you sleep, hugging you, smelling you, sharing moments with you, seeing you smile, hearing you laugh. It would be too much to bear. What was done to you was so horrible, so shocking, but I know that you can recover from it. I know you are strong enough and brave enough. We need you so much, angel.'

This was too much for me. I can handle my pain, I'm an expert, but seeing Jess in such distress, and realising how wrong I had been was excruciating. She wasn't angry at me. She didn't blame me. She was terrified for me. I started crying now. Head in my hands. Unwilling to see anyone. I didn't want to hear any more.

'Josh,' said Kim gently, 'I want you to look at Jess.'

I raised my head a few inches to stare at her.

'You are not toxic,' Kim continued. 'You are not dangerous. You are in a lot of pain and you were damaged by the actions of others to the point where you couldn't bear to live any more. The part of you that wants to die, that wants to leave Jess and Danny, is not your functional adult. It is that little boy who was so badly abused. Who doesn't feel worthy of love, support, understanding and compassion. Can you hear that?'

'No,' I cried. 'That's wrong. They would all be better off without me here. I can't even spend time in the same fucking room as my son. What kind of father does that make me? I haven't been able to be there for my wife for months. What kind of husband does that make me?' I slapped my face as hard as I could to try to stop crying. It didn't work so I grasped a handful of my hair and wrenched it out.

Dr Feinburg leapt into action. 'Okay. I think I'm going to interrupt this now,' he said. 'Josh, I want you to take some deep breaths and look at me.' He crouched down to my level in front of me.

I was sobbing so hard I could barely breathe.

'How old do you feel right now?' he asked.

'About six,' I said.

'Okay. Now I want you to imagine that six-year-old boy. I want you to put him out in front of you and ask him to walk around behind you so that you're in front of him and protecting him. Can you do that?'

I nodded.

'Good. Now, is he behind you?'

'Yes.'

'So he's safe. He's really safe. Now I want you to find the adult Josh and move back into him. Can you do that for me?'

I struggled with it for a minute, but gradually sensed a feeling of calm start to descend. A feeling of growing up twenty-five years in a few seconds. I felt different. More powerful. More solid.

'Okay, Josh. Well done. Let's call it a day for now and I'd like you and Jess to come with me back to my office,' he said.

It felt like a long walk back. I couldn't look at Jess or Dr Feinburg, I just felt so damn small. I was in such turmoil and it reminded me of the feelings I had when I had tried to end it all – feeling like there was no way out but death, like I had been backed into a corner with nowhere to hide and nowhere to run to.

We filed into his office and sat.

'Josh, I'd like your permission to speak openly in front of Jess,' Dr Feinburg asked.

I nodded my consent, still unable to meet anyone's eyes. I could sense Jess and Dr Feinburg looking at me, and I just wanted to be invisible.

'Jess, I understand from Josh that you know some details of his childhood but not all. Josh was sexually abused in the most devastating ways by both his father and a trusted gym teacher. We have found that the earlier the abuse starts, the longer it continues, the number of people involved and the closer their relationship to the victim all contribute to the level and depth of the trauma. In Josh's case all these criteria are at the extreme end and consequently his trauma has had long-lasting and catastrophic effects.

'What I want to explain to you and Josh is how that trauma manifests itself, because I think it will make things clearer for you both. Within Josh there are three distinct personalities: the wounded child, the adapted child and the functional adult.

'The wounded child is the three-year-old boy whose life was turned upside down the moment his father violated him. He has lost any definition of self and fundamentally believes that he is worthless, unlovable and, in Josh's case, actually evil. This is not a flimsy excuse, but rather a belief as certain and as real as knowing that one needs air to breathe. Any child of his age, in order to survive has an inbuilt defence mechanism that forces the psyche to adapt and change in order to deal with the inevitable pressure and disintegration of self that occurs as a result of the abuse. This manifests itself in a number of ways. Dissociation is the first step. In Josh's case he would physically leave his body during the actual abuse, fly out of his bedroom and become numb to what was occurring.

'Obviously he could not maintain that during his everyday life, and so the adapted child manifested itself, at around the age of five or six, in order to protect the wounded child. This adapted child is withdrawn, angry, doesn't trust his caregivers or the outside world, and develops the necessary tools in order to survive what he sees as a permanently hostile and dangerous universe. Again, in Josh's case, this led to him becoming controlling, manipulative, terrified and isolated by the age of six. The longer he was in his adapted child, the more adept he became at survival and his skills at manipulation and control became all the more ingrained. He never grew into his functional adult – the adult who is emotionally balanced, who has a rational view of his reality and the emotional stability with which to deal with life.

'To all intents and purposes his functional adult has never been either present or developed and he grew up in his adapted child, learning to question everything, no matter how innocent.

'This is why he didn't want you to come. This is why he has begged you to leave the marriage, and this is why, ultimately, he has chosen death rather than life. It is not the real Josh who wants those things, rather it is the adapted child, permanently unsafe, always in fight or flight mode, and hypervigilant of his surroundings. He has had enough.

'Does any of that make sense to you?' he asked.

Jess nodded her agreement. 'Sure it does. Now I understand why every time I ask him a question, even something about what film he wants to see at the cinema, he automatically asks "Why?" ' she said.

'How about you, Josh?' asked the doc.

I had listened to everything he had said and it had all rung true for me. He had just spent five minutes describing my entire thought process and outlook on life to a T.

'Absolutely,' I said. 'Jesus. So you mean that the person who begged Jess to leave, who spent years punishing himself, cutting himself, abusing himself, was not the real me, but was a product of invention, a direct result of the abuse? It does seem like a bit of an excuse to me. An easy way out of taking responsibility.'

'Believe me, it is no excuse. The adapted child doesn't want to be loved and nurtured because first he doesn't feel like he deserves it, and second he doesn't believe it is ever genuine. He is always looking for the angles, the hidden motives, the potential for further abuse. He must protect himself against that at all costs which is why, so often, he does it to himself; when you cut yourself you can control the pain, you can decide when to end it, and you can take responsibility for it. You are not powerless over it if you do it yourself rather than have someone else do it to you. That is the great illusion you have convinced yourself of and it has almost killed you.'

Very occasionally I hear or read something and just know with every cell of my being that it is absolutely true. This was one of those times.

'Jess, angel, I think I understand,' I said, looking at her through clear eyes. 'Right now I feel like an adult. Safe. And I know that I want nothing more than to be with you, to love you, to raise a family with you and to grow old with you. It feels true and wonderful. I can't explain it. My head is quiet, I feel secure and strong, and I want to live. I haven't felt this clear in years.'

'And that,' said Dr Feinburg, 'is your functional adult speaking. What we need to do over the next few weeks is to have you realise when you move from functional to adapted, and how you can choose to move back to functional before you act out from your adapted.

'You need a lot more therapy, Josh. I know you want to get home, to be back in London, but I would strongly recommend that you consider going to our extended care facility when you leave here, if only for a little while, so that you can learn more about how to deal with all this. I know from having spoken to Jess before she got here that she too wants you to stay as long as is necessary.'

'I'll do anything you want,' I said, relief pouring over me. I realised that if I could learn to see those parts of myself and be aware of them, then for once I had a real shot at making a decent life for myself and my family.

This was my awakening. I looked at Jess. 'Baby, are you sure you're okay with me staying on a little while?'

'Josh, of course I am. All I want is for you to get better. I had no idea how deep this went. You stay as long as you need to. Just put yourself in their hands; we'll be waiting for you at home when you're ready, I promise.'

We hugged and now I felt it. That feeling of warmth, of love, of hope that perhaps I really did have a chance.

Looking back now I can see that this was the moment my recovery truly started. I had started to reclaim myself, to accept myself, to stop fighting.

Jess left after a truly inspiring week. We had spent the week listening to others going through hell in their relationships and had been taught a great deal about communication and boundaries, the two key ingredients to any relationship. Kim had made it very clear to her that it was me who was responsible for my recovery and that although Jess could support me she should not try to fix me. In fact, if Jess felt I was acting from a place of my adapted child then she was instructed to call me on that and ask me to get back into my functional adult. She was not to try to carry me emotionally and mother me, no matter how broken or fragile I looked.

Jess is tough. She has also endured her fair share of heartache and although she has a huge capacity to give love I know that she understood what Kim was saying. If every time I started to slide down into depression she picked me up and coddled me until it passed, I was never going to get well. This is something I had to reclaim for myself. I was a man and I had everything I needed to accomplish this goal.

Unfortunately my visa only permitted me another four weeks in the US and I needed to get my head out of my ass and throw myself into recovery.

There is nothing a therapist likes more than a patient who is as desperate for help as only the dying can be. Drs Well and Feinburg seemed thrilled with the change in me. I had gone practically overnight from wanting to die to being eager to live and get better, and they knew that I was willing to do anything to achieve that. More importantly, so did I. And this time it was genuine – there was no long-play con going on here. I wanted it bad.

There was a model of recovery running through the Refuge which was repeated in various forms at almost every group session, lecture and meeting. The subject was laminated and plastered all over the walls, photocopied and placed in my welcome folder and brought up all the time by my peers. It was something that I had ignored and avoided during the previous weeks because it just seemed too daunting to enter into, even though this was the very foundation of the Refuge model.

Here's the gist of it, or at least how I interpret it. If you want the full deal you can pay your $60,000 and go yourself.

We are, all of us, born as a perfect, valuable child of God. There is nothing wrong, bad or distasteful about us. Sure we shit, scream and puke but that is because we are 'perfectly imperfect' (a favourite catchphrase of theirs). We are also born utterly vulnerable. We are unable to feed, clothe, nurture, provide for or protect ourselves. We are therefore dependent on our caregivers to meet these basic needs.

We are also, of course, immature. So the five natural characteristics of a child are that they are valuable, imperfect, vulnerable, dependent and immature.

At some point in our young lives trauma inevitably occurs. Now, I know that for me, trauma means sexual abuse, beatings, severe emotional abuse and so on. But the Refuge defines trauma as 'anything less than nurturing'. We all experience trauma to some degree or another, and therefore we all have issues as a result of that trauma.

When that trauma occurs, those natural characteristics turn into dysfunctional survival traits. The valuable child becomes either less-than (a piece of shit) or better-than (grandiose). The imperfect child becomes either bad and rebellious or good and perfect (so one kid goes off the tracks and starts fucking around and doing drugs, while the good child gets straight As and is a model pupil). The vulnerable child becomes either too vulnerable or invulnerable (in other words they become massively over-sensitive or completely walled off and self-protected). The dependent child becomes too dependent ('Don't ever leave me') or antidependent (needless and wantless: 'Do what you like, I'm fine and don't need you or want anyone'). The immature child becomes either extremely immature (chaotic and unmanageable) or over-mature (controlling and emotionally extremely reined in). These traits usually occur while we are still children.

For me, I experienced a serious amount of trauma that was sustained and perpetrated over a number of years. I became less-than (chronically low self-esteem), invulnerable (I must survive on my own), rebellious (drugs and more drugs), antidependent (no one, not even me, is aware of what I need or want) and extremely immature (totally chaotic).

These traits were indeed survival traits. I have no doubt that at the time they saved my life. However, carrying those on into adulthood saw me turn into a man with extreme difficulty experiencing appropriate levels of self-esteem, difficulty setting functional boundaries, difficulty owning my own reality and imperfection, difficulty taking care of my needs, and difficulty experiencing and expressing my reality moderately.

And yet I was married, working, an adult who was expected by society to function as an adult, and, most worryingly, a father who was modelling all these traits to my son. It is no wonder that we pass on our dysfunction from generation to generation – I swore I would not act the way my parents acted to me around Danny. And of course, concerning sexual abuse or neglect I had maintained that oath. What I didn't, couldn't, know was the damage I was passing on to him simply due to the fact that I was totally unaware of my own hidden dysfunction. A pattern of beliefs and behaviours that had become so deeply ingrained from such an early age that I did not even stop to question them.

But it gets more interesting. When the trauma reactions combine with those core issues of self-esteem, boundaries, reality, dependency and moderation, they drive the secondary symptoms of unmanageability which are the ones that pushed me to suicide, drugs, self-harm and depression. Those symptoms include negative control issues, resentment issues and raging, spirituality issues, addiction, depression and physical illness, and intimacy issues.

I heard this and thought about my life so far. I had been manipulative and controlling for as long as I could remember. I was barely containing a simmering cauldron of anger and rage. I had abandoned any kind of spiritual life. I had been addicted to drugs, sex, money, alcohol and food. I was chronically depressed. I had had plenty of physical illness both as a child and as an adult through neglect, abuse and from disowning my emotions. I had never been truly intimate or relational with another human being, least of all with myself.

Things were really starting to fall into place now because together with the wounded/adapted child model, I had a template for understanding my insanity. If my adapted child took over from the wounded child when I was very young in order to protect me and that adapted child did whatever was necessary to survive, then maybe I wasn't evil. Perhaps I wasn't crazy. I wasn't a functional, rational adult who made those decisions to sleep around with older men, manipulate the world and try to kill myself with drugs. I was and am recovering from horrific trauma that drove me to behave and act in ways that made it possible for me to survive. If I was fucked in the ass from the ages of three until ten both at home and at school, the two places that are meant to be safe and nurturing, then of course I'm going to feel like a piece of shit. Of course I'm going to want to try to control every aspect of my life, to lose any concept of something bigger than me in the universe that is there to protect me, to try to blot out my reality with drugs or sex, to have no idea of what it means to be intimate. And of course it provided the most fertile ground possible for my adapted child to grow and dominate my life.

It also went some way to explaining the dark fantasies I had had involving children, something that during that week completely disappeared. Now that I was listening to and nurturing that child inside me, I couldn't begin to entertain the notion of hurting another child, and those desires that had so terrified me were ripped out of me, never to return.

I can't tell you how many hundreds of hours I had spent poring through self-help books and consulting 'spiritual advisers', looking for the answers. Trying to find someone or something to save me. Maybe I just wasn't able to see it before but no one had explained my predicament as concisely and clearly as this.

I took a wrong turn early on in my life and it led me down a road of pain, disease, addiction and desperation. The great fact for me was that the Refuge assured me that I could turn off and find my way back to the path that is right for me.

The following week was to be my last at the Refuge before moving on to their extended care facility which specialised in trauma resolution and provided an invaluable midway step between the sanctity of the Refuge and the sometimes harsh reality of the outside world.

I opened up fully in my groups during that last week, studied diligently during the lectures and shared honestly during my nightly twelve step meetings. It was clear to me and everyone around me that I had been transformed. I was a totally different person to the man who had crawled through the doors seven weeks previously.

Jess and I were speaking regularly on the phone and we continued to share the connection that I so feared had been lost for ever. I could speak to Danny without falling to pieces internally; in fact we had some funny, imaginative and beautiful conversations about dogs, trains, chocolate and dinosaurs. He would ask if I wanted to 'come to mine house for tea?' and I promised him that I would be there soon, knowing that it was true. I was going to get through this no matter what, and finally be able to show up for him.

I was beginning to see him as a little child of God who existed in his own right and not the image of me as a child. I had previously wanted to have the perfect child, in fact I told myself I needed the perfect child and I needed to be the perfect father to that child, otherwise all hell would break loose, but by taking that pressure off myself, and allowing him to be who he was, imperfections and all, I felt much lighter and much more available to him. It was a breathtaking experience.

I started in that last week to get much more in touch with nature, going on walks in the desert, sitting and staring at the trees, the mountains, the incredible birds all around me. I thought back to my admission there, and a long-forgotten quote by Thoreau that my favourite old English teacher had made me learn came into my head:

> *The winter is lurking within my moods,*
> *And the rustling of the withered leaf*
> *Is the constant music of my grief.*

Sure, I was wary of having changed so much in such a short period of time, but there seemed no reason why it shouldn't last, as long as I was doing the necessary work and was constantly on my guard against dishonesty and manipulation.

My last primary group with Dr Feinburg and the others was very moving. He was crying as were most of the group, as they went around one by one and shared their feelings about me and my recovery. Dr Feinburg said that people like me were the reason he did what he did; that I was a miracle and was going to have a lot to offer others in the future. They all shared similar things about my generosity of spirit, my hunger for change and my newfound lust for recovery. He passed around a medallion engraved with the words 'reality, responsibility, recovery' and they charged the coin with love, humility, self-care, compassion, strength and courage.

My gut instinct was (still) to disagree, tell myself that they were lying, that I had somehow faked it and conned them like I had been doing my entire life. But then I decided simply to stop listening to that voice that they called my inner-critic. I realised that it had done nothing for me thus far except to cheapen me, belittle me and depress me. It kept me in the dark where it felt comfortable. It was time to try a new way of thinking and of being. I accepted their words, took them into my heart and allowed myself to feel the joy that they aroused in me. It felt good.

I spent the last couple of days at the Refuge saying my goodbyes and allowing myself to experience the sadness and joy of that process.

During my last peer meeting I graduated, which involved standing up in front of everyone (staff and patients), and saying a few words about what I had got out of the time I had spent there. I cried unashamedly as I spoke.

'My father started raping me when I was still in nappies. My mother ignored it and blamed it on my cute looks. I am today an orphan. I came here to die and I have the scars to prove it. I arrived with no hope, no future and an absolute and unquestionable belief that I was fundamentally flawed and disgusting.

'What I now realise is that you guys are my new family. The friends I haven't met yet are my new family. My beautiful wife and son are my family, and I have been given the strength and courage to pursue life vigorously and honestly. I want to live. I want to be free. And I want to be myself. You have given me that gift and I will never forget you.'

It was a lovely moment and one I hope I will carry with me for ever.

I bought a little notebook and passed it around to my peers and friends there asking them to write a short message to take away with me. One in particular that stands out was the one from Ron, my Survivor's counsellor, who wrote:

> *Josh, working with you and your little boy has been a wonderful experience. I learned a lot; about the human plight, resistance, resilience and the fundamental courage that we have to press on in spite of the darkness. I wish for you some peace and love, tempered with letting go of that which is not yours. May it lighten up your fingers, body and mind so that the wonders of the world and life are like the wonderful music that I make up and you play. Please take care of yourself and have a good life. Happy trails, namaste,*
> *Ron*

I packed up my bags and jumped into the car heading for Freedom House, the aftercare facility that was located three minutes from the Refuge. I had little idea what to expect but I knew I had exactly three weeks there before returning home and I was determined to make the most of that time.

As it turned out, Freedom House was, if it were possible, even more helpful to me than the Refuge. It housed a maximum of twelve people in two large buildings. Each building had a decent-sized living room and kitchen where we prepared our own food. There was Internet access, music was allowed and we were free to come and go as we pleased, provided we attended all scheduled groups and appointments. Even better, we were allowed to eat what we wanted and drink proper coffee. Needless to say, my first trip was to the grocery store and on to Starbucks.

I even surprised myself at Safeway. I had imagined I would go back to eating shit and not giving a fuck about my body, but I bought fruit, salad and plenty of healthy food.

I started doing Pilates every morning and evening and working on getting more connected with my body. I was still smoking like a bastard but felt okay with it. I was just enjoying being myself.

The main difference therapeutically between Freedom House and the Refuge was that although we had two groups each day, we also had three or four individual sessions each week, unlike at the Refuge which was almost exclusively group-based. It also seemed to focus more on a holistic approach. Every morning we had acupuncture before group. And we finished the day with a one-hour meditation at 9 p.m. This was some experience.

The main counsellor was a short, balding Norwegian called Bjorn. He was hugely enthusiastic about all things spiritual, especially meditation, and would introduce us to various different kinds of it each night. My first session was far and away the most bizarre. I had expected a silent hour of reflection and intimacy. I could not have been more wrong.

All twelve of us stood in one of the living rooms, having cleared all the furniture away, and Bjorn outlined what was to happen in his thick Norwegian accent.

'We start with fifteen minutes of shaking, listening to the CD and letting our bodies vibrate and loosen up as we focus on shaking out all the negative energy within us. After this we will have fifteen minutes of dancing. I don't mean dancing like at the disco, but allowing yourself to be guided by your body and spirit in any way that you wish. We will then stand in silence for fifteen minutes and finally lie down in silence for the last fifteen minutes.'

He started the CD and strange hippie-sounding music full of bells and instruments I had never heard before filled the room. We all stood there shaking like epileptics for fifteen long minutes. And then the madness started.

People started dancing in ways I had never seen before. It was the disco from hell: twelve proper mentalists jumping, bouncing, arms waving, heads twisting, groaning and contorting in time with the music. As the only Brit there I tried to hold out as long as I could, but it was kind of infectious. I started nervously moving from foot to foot, swinging my arms a little. Then I just shut my eyes and let go. I danced like a total fucking lunatic and it felt incredibly liberating.

After the last thirty minutes of silence I felt freer, calmer and more in myself than ever before.

The next night was even more profound. We sat and hummed for thirty minutes and then sat still, moving our arms out, palms facing upwards into the universe in one ultra-slow circle lasting fifteen minutes, giving out energy. We then drew in energy pulling our arms back in, palms down, for another fifteen-minute-long circle.

As I was making my circle outwards something remarkable happened. I started to get hot. I mean, seriously hot – forehead sweating, hands boiling. I started to feel a large ball of energy in both hands. It felt like I was holding a balloon filled with water in each hand; just a massive life-force contained within my arms, filling me with love and energy. This happened during each meditation I had there and it filled me with a sense of being connected to something far greater and more powerful than me. If any proof were needed, I felt touched by the presence and existence of a God that was all loving, all powerful, knowable and yet indefinable.

In my head I kept hearing the words 'Wellness, peace, prosperity' over and over again. I don't know where it came from, but what a great affirmation; what else does anyone need?

Before you start thinking I'm some evangelical nut, let me assure you that no one could have been more cynical about this than me. I tried in countless ways to discount, deny and explain away this phenomenon, but I simply couldn't. That energy was there and it was intense and profound. It belongs to all of us and is always available. It filled the hole inside me, and I would be overwhelmed with a sense of serenity and freedom whenever I felt it.

One of the greatest gifts was offered to me during my second week there. We spent that whole week of afternoon groups going through all twelve steps of AA in the way they did it in the 1940s: a back to basics approach that existed before treatment centres and before the misguided idea that the steps were something to do slowly over a number of months or years. In one week we did all twelve of them and the experience for me was earth-shattering.

I fully accepted my powerlessness not just over alcohol, but also over depression and self-harm.

I found and came to believe in a power greater than myself who could restore me to sanity – something that had been long gone from my life. I turned my will and my life over to that power, safe in the knowledge that no matter what happened all would be well; surely a pretty exact definition of faith.

I wrote out a fearless moral inventory of myself, going back over my life and honestly noting where I had been plagued with self-pity, dishonesty, hatred, fear, resentment, self-justification, negative thinking, criticism of self and others, and a whole host of other defects of character. I then read the entire thing out to one of my peers, admitting to him, to myself and to God the exact nature of my wrongs.

That dealt with the first five steps. Steps 6 and 7 asked for me to be willing to have God remove these defects of character and then to ask Him to do so. I could not wait to be rid of them. Like cleaning out a fridge that hadn't been emptied in years, I went in there and with help, guidance and support thoroughly cleaned it out. All the shit that had caused me and others nothing but pain and disillusionment was summarily dumped. It really was that easy. Instead of trying to figure out the 'right' way to live, I just stopped living in a way that didn't sit right with me.

I went back to my inventory and wrote down the names of all those people and institutions that had been affected by my behaviour over the years. I took a small index card for each person and wrote out what harm I had done them, and became willing to make amends to them all (Step 8). I then started contacting them asking if they would be open to receiving amends from me, and if so in what form they would like it – written, by phone or in person (Step 9). I made a firm commitment to follow through on all of them and ask each one what I could do to make it right. As far as Jess goes I can only offer her my heartfelt assurance that I will do whatever is necessary to be the husband I know I can be. Just saying sorry somehow doesn't really cut it with any of the people whose lives I have disrupted. I'm going to need to rebuild their trust and that will take time, which thanks to all of them is something I now have a lot of.

I then turned my attention on how to maintain this new freedom in my life. I learned to take note of my behaviour as it happens and whenever I have been fearful, dishonest, critical or manipulative, to make amends promptly and do what I can to make it right (Step 10).

Every morning and evening I review my day, noticing where and when I have not been true to myself and have behaved outside my value system. I then resolve to do better tomorrow (Step 11).

Finally, I make the commitment each day to carry the message of freedom and hope that I was so freely given to others. Whether that be via a friendly chat, a smile, a small act of service or simply by spending time with someone who needs the company (Step 12).

First and foremost I do all these things not as a chore but because when I do them I have a sense of freedom and dignity that I have never experienced before. They come not from a place of fear but from a place of compassion and love of the self. I am finally and slowly starting to honour myself and the little boy inside me.

And this process is not just about thinking things through and talking about things. There is definite action I need to take to maintain my newfound serenity and peace of mind.

During my many chats with Jess, we realised that we have been living in a way that does not sit right with us. We lived in a £1 million house, over half of which was mortgaged, I drove a £60,000 car in order to try to make me feel important (Christ, I drive maybe 3,000 miles a year – do I really need a car with a TV in it?), we were spending £15,000 for Danny to attend a school that promised to turn him into a proper little mini-banker and his classmates had names like Django and Ophelia, and we were spending money on stuff that was just not important like stupidly overpriced hotels, clothes we didn't need and other similarly unnecessary shit.

Having looked hard at our finances I realised we'd been spending over £8,000 a month just to stand still. We had a houseful of clothes, toys and things we simply didn't need or use. More damaging still, we lived in an area that was filled with my relatives who were openly hostile, not interested in supporting me and frankly dangerous to be around. The thought that I could be walking Danny to school and bump into one of them did not sit right with me or Jess at all.

And so we took action. The universe loves action. It is one thing to think about doing something, to talk about it and plan it. It is quite another actually to do it. We put our house on the market while I was still at Freedom, and within three days had accepted an offer at the full asking price.

Jess found a beautiful flat for us to rent for six to twelve months in a different area of London while we took our time looking for a new, cheaper place to buy. We found a marvellous school opposite the new flat which costs nothing, is highly recommended by every possible educational institution and where my best friend Greg's wife had spent five very happy years. Prayer and meditation are included as part of the curriculum.

I cancelled my American Express card and told Jess that all the stuff we hadn't used in the last six months could be given away or sold on eBay. We also agreed to work on a realistic budget and live a more right-sized life.

Don't get me wrong: money is great and I plan to earn a ton of the stuff, but if I haven't got it right now I can't afford, literally afford, to pretend I have it and to get any of my self-esteem from acting like a big shot when all I feel like is a cunt.

I instructed a car dealership to look at my car and give me a quote for it, and we arranged a meeting for shortly after my return with a dear friend of mine who owns a financial consultancy designed to help families like us live in economic integrity with themselves.

I also called a music dealer in London and sold them my beautiful eighteenth-century cello that had cost me £50,000. I have another much cheaper instrument that is fine for practising and I figure I can always buy another cello when the time is right again. The doctors here have told me that the damage I did to my tendons with the razor blade isn't permanent and I should soon be able to play again at full capacity, which I'm deeply grateful for; one of the first things I want to do is learn a new programme and give some concerts.

Finally I called Ed and got the exact figure he had spent on my treatment. It came to nearly £60,000. Feeling like I was going to throw up, I structured a payment plan that started off with a £20,000 lump sum and continues with a monthly standing order until the entire sum plus interest at 5 per cent is paid off. I wired the first payment this afternoon, something I'm in a position to do now the house has been sold. I have no doubt Ed doesn't need the money. He tells me he doesn't even want it. But it feels right to pay him back what he so freely gave me.

Jess and I have taken big steps to take care of our external life and it feels liberating. But I was also hungry for more work to do on my internal life.

The principal therapy at Freedom House was called Somatic Experience. I had never heard of this before, but it was invented specifically to deal with trauma and Post Traumatic Stress Disorder. Bjorn would sit me down and ask me to close my eyes and focus hard on my body, noticing any pains, sensations or feelings held there.

I would usually notice some ache in my shoulder, or a slight twitching in one of my legs. He'd ask me to focus on that and just observe it. Track it and notice where it went next. He would encourage me to speak to the affected part of my body silently, asking it to relax, reassuring it that there was nothing to be afraid of, that I was here now and was going to take care of everything.

Sure enough my body would relax, the aches would melt away and I would settle into my chair, sinking deep into my own body and feeling utterly relaxed.

He'd then ask me to do the same with my mind, reassure it that I was there to look after things, and that it could relax safely without any fear. My mind would slowly turn into a kind of mental soup, feeling still and serene. We'd then move to my heart following the same process and when heart, mind and body were all relaxed I would move into my very being, my soul, encouraging it to relax and be still and at peace, unafraid and serene.

By the time I opened my eyes we would have been in the process for an hour when I felt like it had been just a few minutes. I'd be lighter, much more aware of my own body and mind, and more energised. It was very powerful, and something I learned easily enough to do alone at any time of the day or night.

The point of all of this meditation, acupuncture and somatic work was to enable me to reconnect with my body. For years I had existed in my head – one of the most dangerous places for me to be, considering the level of distortion and threat it produced. I had shut off entirely from my body to the point where I couldn't tell if I was hungry, tired, sick or even what emotion I was feeling. I also hated my body, especially how it looked. This is an area that is going to take a lot of work and self-acceptance, but one that I'm aware is a vital part of recovery. Almost every shrink I've seen has diagnosed me with an eating disorder. Eating three healthy meals a day, not weighing myself, and not wanting to be so skinny that I'm invisible, is going to be central to living right and recovering.

The plus side of having spent so long in my head is that I'm (apparently) very smart. The downside was that I'm not a real human being at all. I was a kind of robot – a skinny Terminator, always on the lookout for danger. I shared all the physical attributes of a human being – skin, teeth, hair, blood – but inside was little more than a Taiwanese manufactured replica. A pale imitation of myself, and a tourist in my own skin.

The reconnection of body, mind and soul was a process that took effect quickly and effortlessly. Almost as if it had been waiting for me to return home to it and was thrilled to have me back. It was the homecoming that seemed to be the final piece of the jigsaw.

So here I am having finished one journey and started out on the next one. I am waiting for my flight back to London from Phoenix Airport. I have on the same clothes and am carrying the same bag I arrived with nearly three months ago, but there the similarities end.

I have owned my abuse. I have even accepted it. As I left, one of the spiritual advisers there reminded me of something John of the Cross said centuries ago: 'Descending into the depths of my own nothingness, I was then so raised up that I attained my goal.' Insofar as my goal was to stay alive, to face my demons and to choose a more loving, spiritual path, I am comfortable in accepting that I have attained it. I am committed to starting every day with this goal in mind, aware that I have a daily reprieve that is contingent on the maintenance of my spiritual condition. No doubt I'll fuck up, take wrong turns, listen too much to my ego and act out in ways that do not sit comfortably with me, but I will have compassion and an honest desire to notice when I make a mistake and try harder the next day. This is all I can ask of myself.

I feel a healthy degree of fear about my return to London, to family life and to work. I have times where I worry that I will find it difficult to cope with the inevitable pressures of daily life, but I temper that with the certain knowledge that the tools I have learned here really do work; that when I feel the familiar itch of depression and anxiety I can embrace it as a friend and not fight it. I can share my feelings with Jess, with a new therapist in London I've already set up an appointment with and who trained here at the Refuge, and I can be still and enjoy the ongoing mystery of who I am and where I am headed.

I realise that I don't need to know everything and I don't need to control everything. In fact in some ways, the more uncertain I am, the more insecure I am, the better. I know that when I get out of the way and stop trying to orchestrate things to be safe and what I want, then miracles really can and do happen. Jess may decide she's had enough of the chaos and move on, I may run out of money and end up living in a bedsit, I may decide the cello isn't for me and find work in a field I had not previously thought of. On a good day, any of those situations sits okay with me; acceptance is one of the greatest gifts I can give myself. The pain I would feel would be appropriate and manageable, especially if my pride and ego are not involved. Almost every spiritual text I read tells me that only when everything is stripped away from us do we discover who we are meant to be. Money, relationships, status – none of those things will keep me alive and happy, as fun as they can be.

I know for sure that Danny and I are going to forge a new relationship that will be based on love, acceptance, tolerance and faith. That I am going to enjoy the times I spend with him and that I am going to be fully present when I'm with him. I am looking forward to this more than anything. He is charming, funny, smart and mischievous and as he grows up Jess and I plan on encouraging him above all to be himself and to stay true to what he believes in whether or not those beliefs are shared by others or ourselves.

I continue to have no contact with my extended family. I don't expect them to change and I don't expect any kind of amends from them. They have chosen their life and I have chosen mine. They will lose the privilege of getting to know Danny, and I will always have a part of me that is somehow empty. I am open to re-establishing a relationship with my mother because I love her, and I want Danny to have the opportunity of getting to know her, but only time will tell if that is to be, and if it will feel safe enough to pursue. That is my truth and I am okay with it. The abuse I suffered as a child no longer owns me. It has set me free.

I will continue to heal and grow, and no doubt will go through peaks and troughs. For me, today, spirituality is not something to be experienced high up in the mountains meditating or deep in the desert beside bonfires during rituals and ceremonies, enlightening as they may be. Rather it is to be found in the challenges, mysteries and beauty of everyday life: of marriage, children, work and play. Most importantly, it is to be found in love. Big love.

Bring it on.

Acknowledgements

I never dreamed that this would turn into a book, let alone that it would get published. It started out as a suicide note and the fact that it didn't end up as one is down to many, many people. First I owe enormous gratitude to my fearless agent who believed in me since the very beginning and has always put my health at the top of her list of priorities. Also to my editor at John Murray – I knew from our very first meeting that I was in good hands, and her patience, insight and professionalism have been a real blessing. Behind every good literary team there lies a backbone of great support and I'm most thankful to the gang for their work in bringing this book to market.

The real Drs Well and Feinburg, your compassion and patience saved my life; thank you not just from me but also from my son to whom you have delivered a father. To the real Ed, Greg, Pietro, Massimo, Nick and Harry, my dear friends, I can promise you faithfully that I will continue to fight and will show you my gratitude through action, action and more action; you have all given so much to me and my family. God bless you and thank you. To A, the best shrink in town, you have held me and guided me since I came back to London; many, many thanks. And special credit must also go to the musical genius that is Ben Folds for many years of inspiration. Even though I've never met him, his music has provided much solace and inspiration to me.

To anybody who has read this and also suffered the horrors of abuse, I salute you and want you to know that you are not alone; there is a way out. We deserve to be free of the shame that binds us.

And to my wife. The real Jess, I beg your forgiveness, your patience and your compassion. Thank you from the bottom of my heart for helping me to walk through this journey.

Darling Danny. My prince. Daddy has written a book without trains, dinosaurs, Mr Men or Paddington Bear, but it was a book that he needed to write regardless of those unforgivable mistakes. You, my boy, are the greatest miracle and the very definition of love. Each and every time I think of you or look at your beautiful face, I see a million perfect reasons why I will never leave you. I want only your truth and happiness. I will always love you.

Josh Cannon
July 2007